The Elevated Entrepreneur

Unlocking the Secrets of the World's Greatest Coaches, Performers, and Entrepreneurs

Jake Kelfer

The Elevated Entrepreneur

Unlocking the Secrets of the World's Greatest Coaches, Performers, and Entrepreneurs

Jake Kelfer

Cover Design by Jordan Cuellar

ISBN: 978-1-7378283-0-3

Dedication

This book is dedicated to all the entrepreneurs out there hustling to create the life they've always dreamed of.

Table of Contents

Introduction.. 1

What Is An Elevated Entrepreneur? 4

The Book Breakdown 9

Dr. Nicole LePera 10

John Lee Dumas... 15

Jill Stanton... 19

Brandin Cohen..22

Dorie Clark..25

Fancy Isn't Necessary!.. 30

Jon Gordon 31

Lori Harder 35

Anthony Trucks 40

Pat Flynn...42

Alexi Panos 49

How To Handle Rejection As An Entrepreneur 54

Stu McLaren 56

Steve O'Dell 63

Jordan Younger 67

Jay Ferruggia 71

Alison J. Prince 76

Everyone's Got A Million-Dollar Idea . . . Or So They Say 81

Mahdi Woodard 85

Serena Poon 89

Clay Hebert 93

Chris Ducker 99

Allyson Byrd 104

Daily Actions To Be The Best Version Of Yourself 110

Steve Sisolak 113

Ben Newman 116

Rachel Bell 122

Chad Collins 129

Kenzie Burke 134

Mirror, Mirror On The Wall 139

Amanda Holmes 143

Travis Chappell 147

Allie Casazza 152

Steve J. Larsen 157

Tyler J. McCall 161

Jess Glazer 166

The One Thing We All Seek: Freedom!.................................172

Sydney Webb 174

Nick Santonastasso...179

Erik Salzenstein 182

Marley Jaxx..187

Fun Facts About The Guests 191

BJ Fogg 193

Kara Goldin..196

Brock Johnson 199

Kayleigh Christina 204

How To Elevate Further 208

Acknowledgments 209

INTRODUCTION

My name is Jake Kelfer, and if you've never heard of me, here are a few things you should know . . .

I love people. I love winning. I love elevating people to achieve personal greatness. I love the game of life!

Now, before we begin, I want to make something crystal clear. This book is not designed to be like every other book. As a matter of fact, this book is designed to do one thing:

Elevate your ability to be a high-performing, productivity-crushing, and freedom-achieving entrepreneur.

When I set out to write this book, I had three intentions:

1. Elevate my network with people who inspire me and challenge me.

2. Learn from the world's greatest coaches, performers, and entrepreneurs to see what makes them so successful.

3. Share this knowledge with you so you can achieve massive breakthroughs on your entrepreneurial journey.

Over the last few years, I've been on a journey to connect with and interview some of the people I most look up to in the world of entrepreneurship. I've interviewed hundreds and hundreds of people, but this book features some of the best.

There are people featured in this book who I've looked up to since I was a senior in high school, and there are people I met weeks before the book was to be written.

What I've found is when you put yourself out there, provide opportunities that benefit others, and are willing to ask for help, you can accomplish so much. Several of the interviews in this book came from introductions from the other featured guests while others came from cold DMs and messages.

I truly believe that you are one connection away from everything changing!

I hope that this book will inspire you to take action, seek out new connections, and enjoy the journey in your pursuit for greatness.

When I first started as an entrepreneur, I wished there was a book that highlighted some of the best entrepreneurs in the world. Not just that but a book that asked real questions with answers that I could actually take action on.

I am a pretty straightforward person, and I just wanted the secret. What made certain people take off? I wanted a book that compiled information from the best in the world so I could learn and implement rather than making all the mistakes myself. Since I was so new, I wanted to learn from as many people as possible to see what style and approach I liked the best.

Then over a couple of years, Tim Ferriss came out with his books, *Tools of Titans* and *Tribe of Mentors,* and I absolutely loved them and knew one day, I'd write my own interview-style book.

So, shortly after the release of my second book *Elevate Your Network*, I had this idea for an interview book. The idea was to interview people from all walks of life—all backgrounds, demographics, genders, income levels, religions, and more—to see if I could identify the commonalities and differences around success.

I spent hours creating the idea and building out what it could look like. I even started interviewing all types of people with the intention to share their stories because I believe success isn't defined by just money. I believe that every person has their own unique definition of success, and I wanted to find people from all over the world who were successful in their own right.

I wanted to see why these people were successful and what it meant to them.

I interviewed the rabbi who took me to Israel on my birthright trip. I interviewed the Dean of Religious Life at USC. I interviewed a random stranger I met on an airplane from Iowa whose daughter won American Idol. I even interviewed a happiness professor from Harvard.

As time went on and I dug deeper, I realized I needed to get clearer. Just like I tell my clients, I needed to be more specific around who this book was for and the specific result I could provide for them.

After going back and forth, I finally committed to making this a book for entrepreneurs by entrepreneurs. I made a commitment that this book would create immediate results for those who read it, foster new friendships, promote my friends and colleagues, and raise the standard for what it means to be an entrepreneur.

The ideas we have are just ideas. The minute we take action is when everything starts to shift. Most of the time, the initial idea is rarely the final product, and this book is no different. When I think about what I initially wanted to create to what you're reading right now, it's amazing to see the transformation and the growth that happened on these pages and in my life.

That, my friends, is what brings us to this very phrase: The Elevated Entrepreneur.

WHAT IS AN ELEVATED ENTREPRENEUR?

When I was playing for the Lakers, my first-ever basketball team at five years old, I was absolutely terrible as soon as the game started. In practice, I was an animal running around like crazy, but when it came time for me to play in an actual game, I froze. I got shy. I looked like I didn't want to be there.

My parents couldn't figure out why this was happening. It was clear I loved the game. I loved driving to the games, talking about the games, and seeing my new friends.

So, my dad, being the amazing dad he is, tried everything. He asked the coach to put me in the starting lineup to see if that would get me going. When that didn't work, he asked the coach to have me come off the bench because maybe I'd see everyone else running around and jump right in.

Nothing seemed to work. I'd be in the game, and I'd stand right next to the opponent almost as if I was waiting for him to give me the ball like it was a free sample at Costco. It was not a great start for a kid who would eventually dream of playing for the Los Angeles Lakers.

I mean, I was literally afraid to take the ball from the other kids, even though that's exactly what I was supposed to do. I was hesitant to touch them because I didn't want to get a foul; I was trying to do everything I could to not break the rules. I was playing soft!

Eventually, my dad pulled me off to the side, looked me in the eyes, and showed me exactly what I could and couldn't do. He told me that part of the game was taking the ball from the other team and then dribbling it to my hoop and scoring. He told me if the other team threw a pass, I could jump in and steal it.

You see, the hard part for my youthful brain was that my parents raised me not to cheat, not to hurt others, and to be kind. So, in my mind, I probably thought stealing from someone else wasn't allowed. The only problem was I was playing a different game now.

A few minutes after my dad showed me what I was allowed to do, he told me to be more aggressive, that it's okay to get a foul as long as you aren't intentionally trying to hurt someone, and that if I stole the ball, I wouldn't be in trouble. He told me to take charge and go for it, and no matter what, he and my mom would still love me.

That was all my five-year-old, rule-following-self needed to hear.

Almost instantaneously, the light switch turned on. I finished that game as an entirely new player.

Between that game and the next, my parents showed me a few basketball games and what great players did so I could really build off everything my dad shared with me.

By the time the next weekend came around, I was jumping at the chance to get back on the court. From the moment the clock started, I was a completely different person. I was like the Tasmanian Devil in Space Jam, spinning my way around the court getting steals, assists, and lay-ups.

By the end of the game, all my teammates' parents came up to my parents and asked what changed. They could see me stepping into the player I was destined to be.

Over the next thirteen years, basketball became more than just a game to me. It was the sport that pushed me harder than ever before. It challenged me in ways I never imagined. It showed me the power of hard work, discipline, overcoming adversity, leadership, and so much more.

From the time I finished my first season to my last high school game, I played with that same tenacious mentality. I played with a love of the game, always striving to get better. I played to be the very best I could be, and no one could stop me. I played to *win* the game!

Unfortunately, most of us play the game of life like my five-year-old self. We wait for others to tell us what we can and can't do. We wait for permission to go after our dreams. We follow rules that are made up. We live life according to someone else's definition of success rather than our own.

Worst of all, we sit on the sideline watching everyone else do the things we always dreamed of.

But let me tell you something . . .

If you want to win the game of life, you need to get in the game! If you want to win the game of entrepreneurship, you need to start playing. You need to get off the bench and into the game.

We only have one chance to live this life, and every day you wait to go after your dreams is a day you will never get back. Our time here is limited, so it's up to us to decide how we spend it, who we share it with, and what we do with it.

As you read this book, remember that it's not about trying to be like someone else or building a business like someone else; it's about being the best you can be in the game of entrepreneurship.

An Elevated Entrepreneur is someone willing to try, even if success isn't guaranteed.

An Elevated Entrepreneur isn't afraid to go big, despite the fear of being judged.

An Elevated Entrepreneur is willing to do whatever it takes because a life of "oh wells" is better than a life of "what ifs."

An Elevated Entrepreneur isn't afraid to ask for help and be vulnerable.

An Elevated Entrepreneur invests in themselves even when it scares them.

An Elevated Entrepreneur pursues their definition of success relentlessly, regardless of what people think.

An Elevated Entrepreneur enjoys the journey of today while creating the greatness of tomorrow.

An Elevated Entrepreneur takes action to build a life greater than themselves.

An Elevated Entrepreneur is a champion of their own life!

By the end of this book, you will see what it takes to be an Elevated Entrepreneur. The experts featured in this book have achieved incredible success in their own ways; now it's your turn to elevate.

The journey begins now!

I am an

ELEVATED

ENTREPRENEUR

I define my own destiny!
I take intentional action 100% of the time even when it's hard!
I build empires through connection!
I create massive impact!
I connect with the world's greatest people!
I overcome adversity with ease!
I make a shit ton of money!
I elevate the people around me to bring more joy to the world!
I turn dreams into reality!
I get better every day!
I enjoy the journey!
I am fully ELEVATED!

THE BOOK BREAKDOWN

This book is designed to help you achieve personal success on your journey. To make it as impactful as possible, I wrote this in a way where you don't have to read it from beginning to end. It's your journey, so pick and choose what interviews you want to read and when you want to read them. Sprinkled in between interviews are analysis and commentary I created to share wisdom and help you continue to elevate.

Each interview is broken up into three parts.

Part 1 is each guest's bio and social handles so you can learn a little about each person before diving in. This gives you some context about their background.

Here are the codes I used for each social platform:

IG: Instagram
FB: Facebook
LI: LinkedIn
YT: YouTube
TW: Twitter

Part 2 is called How We Met. For this part, I share a quick blurb or story on how this interview came to be. The intention behind this is to share some insight into how you can grow and elevate your network. You will see that some relationships took ten years to get to this point and others took ten minutes.

Part 3 is the actual interview. I interviewed every guest and took the best parts of their interview to share for you. The style is very conversational and casual.

If you want to watch the full video interviews, and gain access to additional bonuses such as freebies and giveaways, you can do so at theelevatedentrepreneur.co/bonus.

DR. NICOLE LEPERA

Bio

Dr. Nicole LePera was trained in clinical psychology at Cornell University and the New School for Social Research. She also studied at the Philadelphia School of Psychoanalysis.

As a clinical psychologist in private practice, Dr. Nicole LePera often found herself frustrated by the limitations of traditional psychotherapy. Wanting more for her patients—and for herself—she began a journey to develop a united philosophy of mental, physical, and spiritual health that equips people with the tools necessary to heal themselves.

She is the creator of the #SelfHealers movement where people from around the world are joining together in community to take healing into their own hands. Her first book, *How to Do the Work*, is currently available.

How to Connect

IG: @the.holistic.psychologist

FB: /the.holistic.psychologist

YT: /theholisticpsychologist

Website: yourholisticpsychologist.com

How We Met

Let me start by saying Dr. Nicole is awesome! She is one of the most influential people on Instagram with 4,000,000+ followers. I love what Dr. Nicole stands for and what she's all about, so I wanted to share her story in this book. The only problem was I didn't know her, didn't know anyone who knew her off the top of my head, and with four million followers, I knew the likelihood of a DM response was going to be tough. Knowing this, I started visiting her other platforms online and learning more about her. Eventually, I found her email address and sent an extremely customized email to her, inviting her to be part of this book. In true Dr. Nicole spirit, she got back to me, and we scheduled a time to make it happen.

I didn't know her before, I didn't get introduced to her, I didn't get intimidated by her massive following, I reminded myself that she is a person just like me and you, and I found a way to get in front of her and provide immediate value.

What is the one thing that, if you knew when starting, would have accelerated your path to success?

I honestly don't think that there is one thing. I think that my own experiences, my evolving, not only personally but professionally, everything that I went through, even the areas that were out of alignment and the work that I'm doing now working holistically is a bit different than how I learned and how I was trained and really how I thought about myself as a human. I think that the growth and the evolution of having to consider some of my old beliefs and work with belief change and integrate healing in the full comprehensive way that it actually takes to transform was all part of my journey. I honestly believe there isn't an answer to that. I think everything that I came to know and I'm still learning informed what I'm doing and will continue to inform what I do moving forward.

No entrepreneurial journey goes from A to B in a straight line. How did you overcome the internal doubts and external adversity along the journey?

That is an evolving, working process. I wouldn't say that I've overcome it; I still have doubts. Each and every time I put myself out there—my ideas, my thoughts, obviously doing so in the realm that is social media—I open myself up to all different types of feedback. That's still very much part of the story for me, and it's a daily process. It's about having my time and my space to drop into what my truth is, aside from all of the messaging and the distraction and everyone telling me what it is they think my truth is, and everything that I think happens really commonly now. Part of the process that I'm describing is dropping into myself, aligning myself, discovering my truth, and staying in alignment with that because doubt is there, so we need to have what I call my home base, and I urge us each to get one where we drop into ourselves so that we can get clarity, so that as we continue to speak our truth amidst the noise and the doubt that is ever present there, we can still maintain connection with what is ours and continue to work to leave what is not.

What is your definition of success?

Empowerment. Learning how to embody ourselves, our truth, our message, our creation, our *us*-ness. I believe that is the most successful endeavor that any human can partake in.

Most people never get started. What would you say to someone who has a dream but is holding back from making the plunge?

There's a lot of reasons we hold back. Change, which you'll hear me talk a lot about in my work, is difficult. We're not evolutionarily actually geared to prefer change because to our subconscious, which is where most of us are operating out of 95 percent of the day, change—the unknown, the possibility of what could happen next—is much more threatening than what we know happens next, even if it's an unfavorable outcome. You'll often hear me talk about change and how it's hard, and how many of us either don't get started and/or we get started a million and one times, and then we don't maintain consistency with change, so we never actually create transformation.

What I would say to people is, it's quite normal to not want to get started, to not want to do unfamiliar things. Again, we're not necessarily geared to comfortably walk into uncertainty, and so as you get started to change, I also would suggest you become aware that there will be difficulty. I call it resistance. That pull, whether it's all of the reasons why we shouldn't do this new thing or all of the ways we convince ourselves out of change, we're just in discomfort of feeling in a new way or being in a new way. Those resistances are part of it.

So, what I would say to people is, resistance to change is normal. It's quite difficult to change; it's absolutely difficult to sustain change. There's an evolutionary reason for that that lives in our mind and in our body, which is why we have to holistically understand ourselves to create change. It's quite normal, and there will be resistance to that change along the way, and none of this is logical, and that's why I talk about it. I think a lot of us carry a lot of shame and a lot of stories about being defective, and this is why we see these patterns. So, I'm here to say it's normal.

How do you relentlessly pursue excellence, greatness, and success (however you define it), while at the same time enjoy the journey of life?

Part of the journey of life or embodying empowerment and us-ness is being alive, is being there for all of the moments. I hate to use these qualifiers—positive, negative, and neutral—all of the things that happen, and that means staying grounded, staying connected to ourselves regardless of what's happening around us, and that's a daily endeavor because we change. Our needs change, our external environments shift and change, and that's why I don't ever believe the answers are outside of us. Empowerment needs to live within, in my opinion, so that we can set ourselves up to succeed, regardless of what's happening around us.

What is one action you recommend someone do every day to be the best version of themselves?

Create a new habit of being conscious of themselves. Most of us, up to 95 percent of our day, are running on that autopilot. Consciousness lives when we're grounded in our body, and the quickest and easiest way to get grounded in our body in the present moment is by using our senses, by doing a senses check-in, and focusing your attention because a lot of us allow our thoughts to drive where our attention goes. Life happens now, so to embody ourselves, we have to learn how to be in the now. What can I see, touch, taste, smell? Chances are, we have one sense that we can activate even if we're just sitting. If I were to just draw my attention from wherever else it was to the physical experience of being in my body against this wall and my cushion right here, now I can be conscious.

While that's the most practical tip, I would go so far as to say that we want to build on that foundation. We want to make one moment many moments of consciousness throughout our day.

How have relationships—personal and professional— contributed to your success and happiness?

They've been everything. From my overall feeling of disconnect from most humans in my life, if not all, starting namely with my mother being emotionally withdrawn because she was anxiously preoccupied with the next stressor. I have a deep sense of lack of relationship, of emotional loneliness, and I think a lot of us have that. A lot of us then engage in seeking patterns to try to grab the levels of connection that we do know we can secure. For me, that was through performance, through serving others, as opposed to just being accepted for me. Relationships are at our core as all humans, and I've experienced the disconnect from all of the emotional pains that come when we limit our self-expression, and we don't feel safe and supported in relationships. We need to feel safe and supported in our relationships so that we can be fully self-expressed. Gradually, I'm evolving, and I've been changing over the course of many years. My relationships are now ones that I can co-create with the other people involved in the relationship—a feeling of safety and security as a container to express myself. For me, it's about finding and engaging most with those relationships where I can be my core self.

Who are three of your favorite entrepreneurs to follow, learn from, and/or connect with?

Gary Vaynerchuk

Gregg Braden

Joe Dispenza

JOHN LEE DUMAS

Bio

John Lee Dumas is the host of *Entrepreneurs on Fire*, an award-winning podcast where he interviews inspiring entrepreneurs who are truly *on fire*. With over 3,000 episodes, 100 million total listens, and over 1.2 million listens a month plus seven figures of annual revenue, JLD is just getting started!

How to Connect

IG: @johnleedumas

FB: /johnleedumas

LI: /johnleedumas

YT: /johnleedumas

TW: @johnleedumas

How We Met

I remember driving to and from my job with the Lakers listening to podcasts for the first time. JLD brought the heat, and I absolutely loved his style and hearing so many stories. I've followed his journey, purchased his products, and when I wrote this book, I knew I wanted to feature him. I asked one of my friends if she would be willing to make the intro for us. She said yes, and within a few weeks, we were on Zoom doing the interview for this book.

What is the one thing that, if you knew when starting, would have accelerated your path to success?

Fake it till you make it is the worst advice you'll ever get. Everybody wants to be like, "oh, I have this accolade and that accolade" right when they start, even if they may not, just because they want people to assume that they're there for a reason, whatever that might be. People want transparency. They want honesty. They want you. They want to be on the journey with you, see your improvements along the way, be part of your team, your tribe, and your family, so it's the worst advice. I would just say the alternative to that, be as completely open, honest, and transparent as you possibly can along your journey; be true to you.

What are three pieces of software/technology you recommend people use in their business?

Schedule Once

Boomerang

TextExpander

For somebody who has dreams of being a wildly successful entrepreneur with freedom, what is the most important thing to focus on?

One thing. What is a massive problem—a real, real pain point in this world—that you can provide the best solution to? Not just a solution to, not just one of many solutions to, but find a real honest-to-goodness pain point and create the best solution to that pain point. That's when you win, period.

No entrepreneurial journey goes from A to B in a straight line. How did you overcome the internal doubts and external adversity along the journey?

I've surrounded myself with the right people. I have a mastermind, and I have an accountability group. These people I know, like, and trust. I respect them, and they are doing great things in the world. They give me support, they give me guidance, they hold me accountable, and I do the exact same three things for them. It's a very tight-knit, close group, and we don't let each other settle for anything less. Everybody needs that in their world.

What is your definition of success?

Success for me is lifestyle freedom. If you can say in the mirror, "I have lifestyle freedom," you are successful in my definition. Everybody has different definitions of success for them, and I respect their definition. Some people want to have a massive team and a huge budget and venture capital and meetings to do, but for me, I moved to Puerto Rico, and I have a five-person team: me, Kate, and three virtual assistants. I wake up every day and my calendar says exactly what I want it to say because I said yes to every one of those things. Usually, and I mean twenty-five days in the month, there's nothing on that calendar. Zero, zip, zilch, and this is by design, and that's success to me. Lifestyle freedom.

How do you relentlessly pursue excellence, greatness, and success (however you define it), while at the same time enjoy the journey of life?

Become relentless at saying no, and most people never understand what that looks like. I say no to almost everything. Now, during book launch mode, I said yes to pretty much everything because I was in promotion mode. By the way, people always ask me, "how do you get the big guests on your show?" I wait till they're in promotion mode because they say yes to everything, but 99 percent of my year of my entire calendar is clear and open except for those couple of days. There's five days per month where I'm grinding. I'm doing interviews for my show, and I'm doing interviews on other shows about five days per month. The other twenty-five days are mine. They're empty, they're clear because I say no to everything. I'm relentless in that pursuit.

What is one action you recommend someone do every day to be the best version of themselves?

Develop the perfect morning. By the perfect morning, I mean, your perfect morning. Everybody's morning is going to be different. Mine updates and shifts and changes sometimes, but I have a perfect morning. I don't successfully execute upon that 100% of the time, but as much as possible, I follow my perfect morning, and I win as a result.

How have relationships—personal and professional—contributed to your success and happiness?

It's been everything. I end every one of my episodes on *Entrepreneurs on Fire* with a quote, "You're the average of the five people you spend the most time with, and you've been hanging out with Jake and JLD today, so keep up that heat." That's a Jim Rohn quote, and it's so true. My connections and my network have elevated my game every step of the way. It's allowed me to not settle for less, but to say, "wow, look at what Lewis is doing in his industry, look at what Pat is doing, what Gary is doing, what Tim is doing." All these people I mentioned, I've now become friends with, and I interact with on a consistent basis, and that's what it's all about. It's about elevating your own personal game, elevating your own personal situation every opportunity you get, and that's what I'm doing. It's not by just grinding and working hard every single day of the week. I had my season of grinding and working, and that season was multiple years back when I first started, and I still have those days now where I am grinding it out. Like I said, an average of five days per month are just complete grind sessions, doing things that I love, exactly like we're doing now, but still putting in the work to get to where I want to be. That's been everything.

Who are three of your favorite entrepreneurs to follow, learn from, and/or connect with?

Gary Vaynerchuk

Tim Ferriss

Lewis Howes

Pat Flynn

JILL STANTON

Bio

Jill Stanton is the creator of Millionaire Girls Club and the co-founder of Screw The Nine To Five (her and her husband Josh's slice of the internet where they help aspiring course creators and coaches quit their jobs, start online businesses, and get past the $100,000/year mark).

Coined by *Forbes* as "a destination for up-and-coming online entrepreneurs," Screw The Nine To Five has inspired tens of thousands of new entrepreneurs to quit their jobs, build thriving businesses, and live lives of meaning and purpose.

When she's not CEO'ing, she can be found traveling the world with her husband, Josh, and their little guy, Kai.

How to Connect

IG: @screwtheninetofive

FB: /screwtheninetofive

Website: screwtheninetofive.com

How We Met

I was scrolling through Instagram looking for some incredible entrepreneurs to connect with. I was trying to find people who I could learn from and people who I could potentially collaborate with. Jill and Josh (aka Screw The Nine To Five) popped up, and I immediately loved their vibe. I did some research and then sent Jill a super personalized DM complimenting her and making a reference to something they always talk about. We exchanged a few DMs, and then I asked her to be a part of the book. A few months later, we locked in a time and did the interview you are about to read. Since we met, she's supported me and introduced me to several amazing entrepreneurs including several in this book.

What is the one thing that, if you knew when starting, would have accelerated your path to success?

Focus on building a customer list and not wasting time creating endless lead magnets and growing an email list of freebie-seekers who don't take action.

For somebody who has dreams of being a wildly successful entrepreneur with freedom, what is the most important thing to focus on?

Simple: get customers and serve the hell out of them.

No entrepreneurial journey goes from A to B in a straight line. How did you overcome the internal doubts and external adversity along the journey?

It's an ongoing process because those thoughts never go away, you just get better at acknowledging them and dismissing them. For me personally, I live and die by a process I use called "catch, cancel, correct." When you notice a negative or disempowering thought come up (and awareness is key for this), you catch it as soon as you become aware of it, cancel it (if you're a weirdo like me, you will legit say "cancel" out loud), and then correct it with a thought you *want* to believe that is supportive and in alignment with who you want to be, what you want to create, and everything you want to experience.

What is your definition of success?

Doing what you want when you want from wherever you want with who you want.

Most people never get started. What would you say to someone who has a dream but is holding back from making the plunge?

What else are you going to do with your time? What I mean is, that time is going to go by no matter what . . . so, how do you want to use it? Do you want to spend it unconsciously because you're too "scared" to try and fail? Or do you want to use it consciously to design a life that means something to you? Because here's the thing, the only reason you're *not* going for it is because you're living in the familiar and you know how to *be* in the familiar. You know how to handle that level of stress, lackluster circumstances, and mediocre results. And anything outside of that is unfamiliar to you. And unfamiliar is scary. We shy away from the unfamiliar because we don't know what to expect and our brains *love* the predictable. So, how can you start making the unfamiliar more familiar to you? And how can you make the current familiar, unfamiliar? What thoughts would you think if you were the person who has everything you say you want? What habits would you have? How would you spend your time? Who would you hang out with? What would you create? Identify that and then start making *that* way of being familiar to you and make the old version of you unfamiliar. Do that consistently, and your whole life will change.

How do you relentlessly pursue excellence, greatness, and success (however you define it), while at the same time enjoy the journey of life?

We prioritize mental white space so that when we are in beast mode, launching, selling, and fulfilling, we are switched on and in flow. When we aren't in that mode, we consciously carve out time to explore the island we're living on, indulge in experiences that fill us up and give ourselves the gift of space so we can be on our A game for people when we're working. Outside of that, we consciously remind ourselves that everything happens *for* you, and that life is neutral, and the only meaning it has is the meaning *you* give to it.

How have relationships—personal and professional— contributed to your success and happiness?

I believe business is built on relationships. Fortunately, one of my strengths is connecting with people and building relationships. So, for me, it's pivotal that I make it a point to connect with people, jump on calls, do interviews, go to live events, join coaching programs, and put myself around people who match my future. Some of my most meaningful relationships are with people I've met through investing in things like coaches, live events, and masterminds, so I am a big believer in cutting checks to go faster and surrounding yourself with people who are where you want to be.

BRANDIN COHEN

Bio

Brandin Cohen is the founder of Liquid I.V., which was acquired by Unilever in a blockbuster acquisition in October 2020. Now, he's continuing his mission to change the world and help people live better lives for generations to come.

How to Connect

IG: @brandin_cohen

LI: /brandincohen

How We Met

When I was running the Pro Basketball Combine, my friend Jake Kassan (co-founder of MVMT) introduced me to Brandin because he thought we'd hit it off. He was 100% right. We immediately bonded, and Liquid I.V. sent product for our player swag bags. Brandin is one of those people who is out to change the world, so to share his message with you all is a true blessing.

What is the one thing that, if you knew when starting, would have accelerated your path to success?

I think understanding that no matter how good of an entrepreneur you are or how good of a plan you have or how good of a team you have, you're going to go through a lot of peaks and valleys. I really lived and died with those, and I think if I could have—as I got further in the business—realized that no matter how good the business is going, there are always going to be these waves in the business. I equate it to sitting on the riverbank and the river's going by. In the beginning of the business, I would always be swept away in the river, and I think as I got more accustomed to that, I could sit on the riverbed and watch the river go by and observe things that were happening and not get so affected by them.

For somebody who has dreams of being a wildly successful entrepreneur with freedom, what is the most important thing to focus on?

The main one I would say is just to get started. I've talked to so many entrepreneurs who reach out, and there's just all these reasons that they don't start. Whether it's financially or they have another job or they're in school or their family doesn't want them to, you need to plan and to be thoughtful, but nothing happens without starting. Starting is the momentum you need to make your craziest dreams come true, so I think starting is the one thing that I constantly see people struggle with. Just put one foot in front of the other and get going.

What is your definition of success?

It's having the biggest, most positive impact on the world and people as I can while I'm alive. I want to be the best version of myself, so I can inspire people to be the best versions of themselves. I want to bring people together in a world that is really quite divided, and I want to leave a lasting impact on the world. When I'm making decisions on what I want to do next or the businesses that I want to invest in, it always has those parameters. To me, it's always about impact. If you follow impact and purpose, money follows. I've never been driven by money, and I've learned that over the last year as we got acquired. It's never been what inspired me. It's always been impact. I think if you think about the things that are going to have the biggest and most positive impact, the money always follows.

How do you relentlessly pursue excellence, greatness, and success (however you define it), while at the same time enjoy the journey of life?

I really struggle with that. For five or six years, I didn't. I enjoyed the grind, I enjoyed the struggle, but I wasn't smelling the roses at all, and I think as I've gone on to this next phase, when I have a little time to breathe and comprehend everything as I move on to my next venture, a big part of it is that I need to be in a good spot personally which includes my routine, my health routine, what I eat, and my social life. When that's all in a good place, I'm a better leader, I'm a better entrepreneur, and I'm a better innovator. It's a constant practice. This is not something I'm very good at at all. Naturally, I'm just obsessive about what I do when I care about something, and so it takes a lot of discipline and awareness and consciousness to not have tunnel vision.

What is one action you recommend someone do every day to be the best version of themselves?

I think everyone has to figure it out for themselves because we're all so different. For me, routine is probably the most important thing. I've become obsessive with my routine and that structure allows me to have these pockets of creativity and innovation and thinking outside the box, but that only comes within a really strong structure of meditation, yoga, working out, family time, good food, healthy diet. Then when I have all that set, I have this foundation which is a launching pad for my biggest idea, my best execution, and my best relationship building.

How have relationships—personal and professional—contributed to your success and happiness?

The biggest factor in all of our success or accomplishment has been relationships. Over my whole career, it wasn't a strategy, it was just me being me. I loved building, and I loved connecting with people. As we built the business, those relationships are what I called on in order to keep growing it, and now people do the same with me as well. I would say really, really great relationships are such a massive part of our growth, whether it's employees or investors, retailers or family. Having a relationship with yourself is a huge one that I constantly work on as well. All of those are what played such a major factor in our growth.

Who are three of your favorite entrepreneurs to follow, learn from, and/or connect with?

Justin Kan

Martin Luther King Jr.

DORIE CLARK

Bio

Dorie Clark has been named one of the Top 50 business thinkers in the world by Thinkers50. She is a keynote speaker and teaches for Duke University's Fuqua School of Business. She is also the author of *Entrepreneurial You, Reinventing You,* and *Stand Out*, which was named the #1 Leadership Book of the Year by *Inc.* magazine. A former presidential campaign spokeswoman, she writes frequently for the *Harvard Business Review*.

How to Connect
IG: @dorieclark
FB: /dorieclarkauthor
LI: /doriec
YT/Clubhouse: /dorieclark
TW: @dorieclark
Website: dorieclark.com/entrepreneur

How We Met

I first heard of Dorie several years back and was super impressed, so I tried to reach out to her. I followed her on Twitter, joined her email list, and started to engage. Shortly after, I connected on LinkedIn, and we set up a time to chat. Over the past couple of years, we've stayed in touch sporadically, and when I decided to write this book, I invited her to be a part of it. After several back-and-forth messages and being flexible with timing, we were able to make it work. This is the power of following up, updating your connections, and being persistent.

What is the one thing that, if you knew when starting, would have accelerated your path to success?

I think the number one thing was I did not appreciate—at all—the importance of email lists, and that is something that has become really critical to my business. Now, I watch it like a hawk and try to cultivate it, but especially as social media becomes noisier and noisier, and of course, these are publicly traded companies that are incentivized to constantly dial back your access to your followers unless you're paying to play, an opt-in email list becomes a more and more valuable asset every day. Focusing on building, cultivating, and creating your email list is one of the best ways to ensure your relationship with your customers and also your own economic future.

What are three pieces of software/technology you recommend people use in their business?

ConvertKit

Neewer ring light

Microsoft Word transcription

No entrepreneurial journey goes from A to B in a straight line. How did you overcome the internal doubts and external adversity along the journey?

A lot of my external rejections ironically happened even before I was an entrepreneur, and they actually helped set me on the path to entrepreneurship because there were probably three major professional setbacks. The first was that I originally thought I wanted to be a college professor. I completed a master's degree and then applied for doctoral programs, and I ended up getting turned down by all the doctoral programs I applied to. Then I decided I would become a journalist, which is kind of similar. There's reading, there's writing, and all those kinds of things. I got a job as a journalist, and then within a year, I got laid off from the job, and there was a big recession. I can't get another job as a journalist, and then it turns out it's not just a recession. It's actually the news industry is collapsing, so I can't be a journalist. Then I worked in politics because I had been a political reporter, so I was able to transfer the skills. I worked for two campaigns, and both of them lost, so I was striking out all over the place. Ultimately, I became an entrepreneur, and in some ways, it felt smoother sailing at that point because I knew that as long as I didn't quit, nobody else was going to fire me, which felt reassuring.

In terms of overcoming doubts, it was very frustrating and upsetting in all of those cases that the plans that I had made or the outcomes that I would hope for were not going to happen and were not going to materialize. I think that in general, I am pretty good, for better or for worse, at contextualizing and saying that I did my part, and I worked my hardest. I think that it's important to separate out things you can control and things you can't control and be gracious with yourself if you legitimately feel like you tried your hardest. I knew I did, so I wasn't going to take this as the judgment of the universe that I was somehow lacking. I did what I could do, and it didn't break my way, so I tried something else. Eventually, something's going to work.

What is your definition of success?

My definition of success is about self-actualizing. It's about maxing out whatever your individual version is. There's a quote attributed to Abraham Lincoln I really like that says, "Whatever you are, be a good one." If you're a janitor, great. Be the best and be a great janitor. The same goes, whatever your vision is, max it out.

Most people never get started. What would you say to someone who has a dream but is holding back from making the plunge?

One of the most important things that we can do is find ways to lower or mitigate the risk. Some people are actually not necessarily wrong to not go into entrepreneurship because they have set up circumstances for themselves through their life choices where they have no margin for failure. If you have the proverbial golden handcuffs where you've got the kids in expensive school, and you have a mortgage, and it is strictly reliant on a corporate salary, it's very hard to leave because almost certainly, you're not going to be making that amount of money out of the gate. Just about everybody understands it takes time to build up an entrepreneurial venture, so it may not actually be the smartest move.

Now, that being said, the big problem in that circumstance is that people think that is a safe circumstance. They think it's fine because they've got this money coming in. The big problem comes when suddenly, one day, unexpectedly, the money doesn't come because you get laid off or there's a disruption or a merger or a problem in some way, and then it becomes extremely perilous. What you can see when you're on the other side of it is actually being an entrepreneur is far less risky because your business is diversified. You have multiple clients, and you may have multiple income streams, so any disruption is fundamentally much less likely to alter your lifestyle. It actually starts with getting yourself in a position so that you can afford to take risks, and that is an uncomfortable thing for many people. It may mean taking the kids out of private school. It may mean selling the house or downsizing to a smaller one, and people just might not be willing to do it.

For me, when I was getting ready to start my business, I bought a house, but I deliberately bought in the poorest, cheapest neighborhood in my town. I did it because I never wanted to have to be in a position where I feel pressured about money or where I feel that I have to do things for money that I didn't want to do. I knew with the mortgage I had and the payments I had that I could pretty much always manage it without a problem because I did not purchase above my means, I purchased below my needs.

How do you relentlessly pursue excellence, greatness, and success (however you define it), while at the same time enjoy the journey of life?

I would say it's sort of two pronged. The first is being fairly relentless about prioritization and making sure you're working on the most impactful things. I try hard to answer the question upstream about what is the most valuable thing that I can be working on so that I'm not frittering the time that I do spend.

The second piece comes from a lot of interesting research, notably done by Tony Schwartz, author of *Manage Your Energy, Not Your Time.* It's basically just prescribing more awareness about your physiology and how it ties in with your productivity. I try to be mindful of matching the times when I'm best able to do certain work with my circadian rhythms. I know when it starts to get into the evening, and I've been on Zoom for twelve hours, I just know that there are diminishing returns. I can try to do whatever, but it's not going to be that impressive. Sure, I can make myself sit there for another four hours and bang something out, but whatever that thing is, I could probably do it in an hour if I did it the next day. I think part of it is being aware of your body and knowing when to call it a day and when to shift into something else.

How have relationships—personal and professional— contributed to your success and happiness?

Relationships certainly have been critical to the work that I do, both in terms of making it more enjoyable and in terms of leads that I've gotten and collaboration opportunities. One thing that I started doing a fair amount of this year, largely because it's a nice way to work with people, even from remote when you aren't seeing a lot of people, is I started co-authoring a lot of pieces.

Also, some of the fun things that I've done in my life have been relationship driven. I invest in Broadway shows, and I roped in my friend Alisa Cohn to join. We have an LLC together, and we have invested in four theatrical shows together. I have another friend named Kabir Sehgal who brought me in on a project that he was working on. He's very involved in the jazz world, and he brought me in as an assistant producer on a jazz record which won a couple of Grammys. When we won the Grammys, I got to go and be up on stage, which was amazing. I got to have the opportunity through my network to be a producer on a Grammy award-winning album, which was pretty cool.

Who are three of your favorite entrepreneurs to follow, learn from, and/or connect with?

Seth Godin

André Chaperon

Russell Brunson

FANCY ISN'T NECESSARY!

One of the questions I asked almost every guest was **"What are three pieces of software/technology you recommend people use in their business?"**

I expected to hear some fancy, high-tech software that was only accessible to the greats or people with huge budgets and businesses. I expected most people's tech stacks to be super elaborate and expensive. I expected them to have some super special secret that's only available to certain people.

I couldn't have been more wrong.

Every single expert mentioned at least one software that is free and/or available to every single one of us. These experts could have answered with any piece of software or technology they wanted, and every single one of them answered this way.

As entrepreneurs, we tend to overcomplicate things.

We make things harder than they have to be because it's what we think all the experts are doing or it's what we think will get us to the next level. By doing this we make it harder than it needs to be, which ultimately slows down our productivity, focus, and growth.

We think that complexity is what we need in order to be elite, but in reality, less is more. The best in the world know that to win, you need to make things simpler.

Among the most popular answers for this question were technology and software related to basic communication, organization, task management, and productivity. This isn't by accident.

Elevated Entrepreneurs understand that time is money. By focusing on what needs to get done and by doing it in the most efficient way, they are able to achieve more in a day than most. This gives them a huge advantage, and over time, this is what creates a gap from those that skyrocket and those who make incremental progress.

JON GORDON

Bio

Jon Gordon's best-selling books and talks have inspired readers and audiences around the world. His principles have been put to the test by numerous Fortune 500 companies, professional and college sports teams, school districts, hospitals, and non-profits. He is the author of twenty-four books including eleven best sellers and five children's books. His books include the timeless classic *The Energy Bus,* which has sold over two million copies, *The Carpenter*, which was a top five business book of the year, *Training Camp, The Power of Positive Leadership, The Power of a Positive Team, The Coffee Bean, Stay Positive, The Garden, Relationship Grit,* and *Stick Together.* Jon and his tips have been featured on The Today Show, CNN, CNBC, The Golf Channel, Fox and Friends, and in numerous magazines and newspapers. His clients include The Los Angeles Dodgers, The Atlanta Falcons, Campbell Soup, Dell, Publix, Southwest Airlines, LA Clippers, Miami Heat, Pittsburgh Pirates, Truist Bank, Clemson Football, Northwestern Mutual, Bayer, West Point Academy, and more.

Jon is a graduate of Cornell University and holds a master's in teaching from Emory University. He and his training/consulting company are passionate about developing positive leaders, organizations, and teams.

How to Connect

IG/TW: @jongordon11

FB: /jongordonpage

LI: /jongordonenergy

YT: /jongordonselects

Website: jongordon.com

How We Met

During my high school basketball days, I came across the book *Training Camp*. It was one of the first personal development books I read after *How to Win Friends and Influence People*, and I absolutely fell in love with the book. Since reading it, I've had a quote from the book hanging in my room for over a decade. The way Jon and I got connected for this interview was through Coach R-Jay Barsh, who originally reached out to me to work the Pro Basketball Combine when I first started the event. Our relationships grew and after four years, he made the introduction to Jon which brings us to the following interview.

What is the one thing that, if you knew when starting, would have accelerated your path to success?

I wish I would have learned about building a back end early on in terms of having different programs and training and workshops to support the work you already do, but I also believe that that was something that had to take time for me to understand how to help others. When you do a keynote or you do a speech that will shift a lot of people, it will encourage people, it will make a difference for some of the people, but others need more implementation. They need the principles ingrained, they need to actually do the implementation work over a year, and that's where they need workshops and training. Over the years, I've developed workshops and training to actually do that, but early on I did not, so I probably made a good impact, but not as big of an impact as I could have if I would have known that there are some people that don't get impacted by the first talk and they need more.

What is your definition of success?

Success is the fulfillment of God's plan for your life. Are you living this plan? Are you doing what you're called to do? Are you living your purpose and what matters most, and focusing on that because if you're not it doesn't matter how much money you make? It doesn't matter what you do. It doesn't matter how many cars you have. What matters is, did you live the purpose that you had for your life? To me, that is success.

Most people never get started. What would you say to someone who has a dream but is holding back from making the plunge?

Telescope and microscope. You have to have this big picture vision of what you want to create, but you also have to have the zoom-focused actions in order to create that picture in the telescope. So, you need both. Vision, but then zoom focus. Action, taking action each day. The bigger question is, why aren't you taking action? What's holding you back? You have to examine that and look at that. Most often it's fear, fear of not being able to be successful, fear of not getting things done, fear of If I fail what does that say about me and who I am. We know that successful people never consider themselves a failure because when they fail, it's just an event not a definition, but I think so often people are so fearful of what might happen and what it says about them that it's easier not to take action.

How do you relentlessly pursue excellence, greatness, and success (however you define it), while at the same time enjoy the journey of life?

You're not always going to enjoy every day of the journey. There are days that you don't enjoy it, but you do want to bring joy to what you're doing. You don't want to go through life with a clenched fist and a frown on your face. You want to make sure that you are enjoying the ride as I wrote about in The Energy Bus.

Grit is inspired by vision and purpose. Where am I going? Why am I going there? We don't get burned out because of what we do, we get burned out because we forget why we do it. We have our vision, we have our purpose, and then along the way through the adversity, through the challenges, we keep our vision alive, and we keep our purpose going. Our purpose is greater than our challenges and our vision is greater than our circumstances. If you love the process, you will love what the process produces, so you have to make sure you love that process, and that's where the joy comes in. A lot of times entrepreneurs and people want to be successful, but we allow the fear of failure to hold us back, we allow the fear to steal our joy, and we compare ourselves to others, so we lose joy that way and allow all of these things to get in the way. If you just focus on what you're doing and why you're doing it and the love you have for doing it, that's where you bring the joy and fulfillment along the way, even through the tribulations, the challenges, and the setbacks. I'm not going to love every day, but I'm going to love what I'm doing.

How have relationships—personal and professional—contributed to your success and happiness?

If you don't love it, you'll never be great at it. It's the people you love and who love you that allow you to be successful. It's all about relationships. I wrote a book with my wife called Relationship Grit which came out during the pandemic when a lot of people were struggling. I asked my wife, "On a scale of one to ten, how much do you like being married to me?" She said, "pre-COVID or now?" And so, we had to actually use the principles in the book during that time to build a stronger relationship through it. The relationships that you have ultimately determine who you are and the success that you create. If I wasn't a great husband, if I didn't have a great relationship with my wife, we would not be together, and my life would be so different. I wasn't a great husband early on, and so if I didn't change, I would have been divorced, and so where would my life be at this point? Who would I be? I know who I am, and I know that who I am is better because of her. I know the people I've met along the way, the coaches I've worked with, the teams I've worked with, the companies I've worked with, the leaders I have met on my journey, have made me a much better person and a much better leader. I wrote The Power of Positive Leadership with all these great influences in my life that I've had the opportunity to work with and by working with them, I learn from them. It's the relationships that I've built along the way with people that have also helped me grow: my kids, team of speakers, trainers, consultants. These are incredible people that I've had the opportunity to work with, and I know I'm better because of them. No one creates success alone. We all need a team to be successful. We are better together and together we accomplish amazing things. To me, it's all about relationships.

LORI HARDER

Bio

Lori Harder has built three separate seven-figure businesses. She is the founder and CEO of Lite Pink, a new lite rosé flavored wine seltzer that helps women connect, collaborate, and celebrate better. She is a best-selling author of A Tribe Called Bliss, the founder of The Bliss Project event, runs the Forbes' Top 18 female-led podcast Earn Your Happy with over twenty-eight million downloads, and co-hosts the new podcast Girlfriends & Business launched alongside Alli Webb (founder of Drybar) and Brit Driscol (founder of Squeeze). Her career started in the fitness industry as a three-time fitness world champion, eleven-time fitness cover model, and gym owner. As a top seven-figure earner annually in network marketing, this revealed her true passion for helping women grow their businesses, which led her to create her own online courses and educational entrepreneur events. She resides in Scottsdale, Arizona, with her husband, Chris, and dog, Bananas.

How to Connect

IG: @loriharder & @drinklitepink

How We Met

I've been hearing Lori's name for years but never had a chance to connect with her until now. To make this interview happen, I was introduced by Jess Glazer via IG DM. Since intros are one of the best ways to make something happen, Lori and I were scheduled to talk within a week of being introduced. The power of an intro from a reputable source can be the difference in collaborating or never meeting someone. I am so grateful that Lori was willing to make this happen during a crazy productive time for her and her business.

What is the one thing that, if you knew when starting, would have accelerated your path to success?

Hire people better than you before you're ready for it. I think that I would have somehow tried to create a little more money in my business so that I could either afford them or have the faith that the things that they do are going to bring me a much larger profit from the get-go instead of having new people practice on you and pay for their learning and mistakes. There's a time and a place for that, but it is a game changer when you hire people better than you, and it can be scary. As an entrepreneur, I'm definitely in that place right now where I'm thinking these salaries are big, but I can't afford to hire someone who doesn't have experience launching companies like this.

What are three pieces of software/technology you recommend people use in their business?

Asana

Dropbox

Slack

For somebody who has dreams of being a wildly successful entrepreneur with freedom, what is the most important thing to focus on?

I think you need to know that there are seasons. You need to know what season you're in, and you have to put an end to the season, meaning you have to make sure there's either a goal or that you work in some sort of vacation or you work in some time off for you or your team. I think seasons are really important.

Also, question everything. That's actually the season I'm in because I look at all of these female founders, and Chris and I want to start a family, and a lot of people are telling me I'm not going to be able to start a family when I start a company, or I'm not going to have any time, or I'm going to be so burned out. I'm really questioning if that's true for me, meaning "Does it have to be that way? Who could I put in place so that I could actually create some time in order to do that?" Maybe it's not right now during launch, but maybe it's next year or two years from now, and really asking myself how I can have a different story, and if that's just something I believe because I see it with everyone else, or if I can look for other examples.

So, I would say you need to find some examples of people living a full life with freedom. See what they're doing, what they build in, and what they allow in their life. Danielle LaPorte talks about a quote where she says, "Everything on your plate is there because you asked for it or you put it there. You said yes to it." Get really clear on what you are saying yes to and asking if you actually need that thing or need to do that thing in order to move your business forward.

One more thing is looking at your goals and seeing if your goals are actually what you want. Sometimes we throw these numbers out because we want them and someone else hit them, but really being like, wait, we just realized that half of that would actually get us the dream life that we want while allowing us to have time. Evaluating your goals is huge, and then working with those numbers and actually adding up what it looks like to live this dream life and have these things you desire. See if that number actually matches this number that you set for these goals, and if not, then you don't have to work as hard.

What is your definition of success?

It's different all the time. I was going to say success without feeling happy really isn't successful, but I have to tell you, sometimes I think there are times in your life where happiness doesn't equal success. I know that's so counterintuitive, but there was a time in my life where I was so far from doing tough things, that I needed to learn discipline, desperately. I had never completed anything. I was homeschooled through high school. I was raised in a more restrictive family growing up, so the second I moved out at eighteen, I went crazy. I was doing everything I wanted to do, which was not working for my life at all. I was so undisciplined and got myself into a really bad place, so doing all the things that I thought were going to make me happy were making me miserable, and I knew that I needed to do some tough things. I needed to prove to myself that I could finish something because at the time, I had never finished any project or thought or hobby or idea I ever started in my entire life.

I adopted this mantra that I finish everything. I had to complete projects. I had to see things through. I was really uncomfortable everywhere in my life from meeting new people to working out to not going out anymore. I equated happiness to drinking and going out, and I wasn't doing that, so I felt really unhappy. But I was learning discipline, and I was learning delayed gratification, so that was success for me. I was feeling freaking miserable for a while, and that was really successful. I think that sometimes we can get it really misconstrued. I think there's a good balance, and when you learn those habits, you learn who you are, and then you really can start asking yourself what really makes me happy. How do we make sure that I weave that into this project that I'm doing or this big goal that I'm trying to accomplish? I've done so many big goals without weaving those things in, and I'll tell you, it's great in the beginning, but then it starts to not be worth it, and you don't understand why you're working that hard. It starts to become miserable and meaningless, and I think it is important to understand the season I am in and ask if I need to learn some freaking discipline.

If I'm feeling challenged, if I'm feeling content in a lot of areas of my life, if I'm growing, if I really love who's around me and they're elevating me energetically, that feels like success to me. I already feel successful with my company, even though it hasn't started. I feel successful because I'm sticking to what felt aligned for me when I started this, so I'm listening to my gut and I'm listening to myself, and that feels like success right now.

What is one action you recommend someone do every day to be the best version of themselves?

Take a walk with a good question in your head. Not a disempowering question but a good question. How can I do this? Who would I need to talk to? Who do I need to be to make this happen?

How have relationships—personal and professional— contributed to your success and happiness?

Relationships have been everything. I would not be where I am right now. I would not even feel this level of contentment. I wouldn't feel this level of excitement if it weren't for who I get to work with and who I've gotten to work with.

I literally came from a religion where I wasn't allowed to hang out with anyone outside of the religion to coming into a world where I knew no one and did not have anyone or any friends who were in the entrepreneurial world. None of that came until my early thirties when I started seeking it out. I paid for all my friends and mentors in the beginning, meaning I met them all in masterminds where they paid too. That was huge for me because I needed to get into places where people had a different mindset and where things were being facilitated and taught in a different belief system. Without all those relationships, I would have never changed what I believed was possible for myself.

Who are three of your favorite entrepreneurs to follow, learn from, and/or connect with?

Bill Glazer

Rob Dyrdek

Jamie Kern Lima

ANTHONY TRUCKS

Bio

Anthony Trucks is a foster kid turned NFL athlete and serial entrepreneur with one serious superpower: Making Shift Happen, no matter what, by accessing the power of identity. After overcoming over thirty traumatic life events and navigating the identity shifts that followed, Anthony has come to be known as the leading expert in "Shifting," which is making a shift internally to elevate how you operate externally. This, in turn, changes your life. With his unique coaching system called "The Shift Method," Anthony weaves together neuroscience, psychology, technology, and hard-fought life lessons to help anyone with a desire for more in their life achieve any goal they want or have ever wanted. Before making it apparent their goals were actually set far below their true potential in the first place. Buckle up. It's time to Make Shift Happen

How to Connect

IG: @anthonytrucks

Website: sloworgo.co

How We Met

In 2019, I attended Brendon Burchard's Influencer conference in San Diego. I heard Anthony speak on stage and was blown away with his story, so I knew I needed to find a way to get to know him. At the conference, I posted an IG story and tagged him on stage. Following the conference, I used one of his quotes in a takeaway post. Shortly after, I reached out via IG and shot him a message. We jumped on the phone and a few months later, I flew to his place and interviewed him for this book.

What is your definition of success?

I find that success is peace and loving the journey. A lot of times, I have this goal that I have to get this and buy this and make this thing, and then I find that I'm not at peace. I'm always fighting to get this thing, and when I get this thing, it's never as enjoyable as I think it could be.

Success is enjoying the trip and then when I get to a destination, whether it's good or bad, it is what it is. Success for me is peace and not having a lot of unsettled stuff in life, so I just enjoy my life. Success is also control. I don't think it's freedom. Freedom says I'm free to make a choice, but the choice could be: do I want to go to this job I hate or this job I don't hate? Whereas control says, I control what my life is and how it operates. So, for me, success isn't a bunch of money. It isn't a bunch of notoriety. It can be someone that nobody knows but has control of their life. Maybe it's a guy that has a plot of land up in the middle of nowhere, and he lives completely in his own little world. He's successful to me. He has control. Success to me is peace and control.

How have relationships—personal and professional—contributed to your success and happiness?

100%. There's nobody self-made. When you were a kid, somebody fed you and took care of you. You would have died if someone didn't take care of you. You weren't self-made. Now, there's certain things you may have done that other people didn't, but you had to have been in a conversation or someone had to give you information, insight, guidance. At the end of the day, you have to have relationships in your life that mean something because whenever we get a chance to win, it sucks to celebrate in quiet and silence. When I was playing in the NFL, you had a team to celebrate with. It's great to win, so the relationships have always contributed, whether it's a mentorship relationship or a support relationship. I serve my clients, and I love those relationships. I have a coach, and he serves me, and I love the relationship. I have my wife, I have my kids, and all of those things bring different senses of accomplishment and joy and giving and caring that you can't get by yourself. You can't gift yourself something that feels as good as if you gift somebody else something, so the relationships are the driver and the reason why I do what I do. We as human beings are created to be in relationships. It's why we can communicate. We're designed to be with other people and have great relationships. It's the root of everything we do.

PAT FLYNN

Bio

Pat Flynn is a father, husband, and entrepreneur who lives and works in San Diego, CA. He owns several successful online businesses and is a professional blogger, keynote speaker, *Wall Street Journal* best-selling author, and host of the *Smart Passive Income* and *AskPat* podcasts, which have earned a combined total of over sixty-five million downloads, multiple awards, and features in publications such as *New York Times* and *Forbes*. He is also an advisor to ConvertKit, LeadPages, Teachable, and other companies in the digital marketing arena.

How to Connect

IG: @patflynn

YT: /smartpassiveincome

TW: @patflynn

Website: patflynn.com

How We Met

Pat was among one of the first online entrepreneurs I ever heard of. His blog and podcast, Smart Passive Income, taught me so much when I was first being introduced to this world. Over the past five years, I've watched from afar and implemented his teachings. He was one of the first people I thought of when I started writing this book, so I thought about who I knew who was connected with him and asked my friend to connect us. Shortly after, I put the dots together, Chad Collins made the intro, and put us in touch.

What is the one thing that, if you knew when starting, would have accelerated your path to success?

The more people you're able to connect with and serve, the more successful you'll become. I wouldn't be where I'm at today without the people I've been able to connect with. You might not know, but the next person you meet at that event or on a Zoom call or in a virtual event, wherever it might be, could be the person who connects you with exactly who you need or could be that person. They could have the ability to tell you about all the mistakes that they made so you don't have to make them too. There are people out there in the world who've experienced way more than any of us have, but when you find the right people, they can help guide you, and it can help inspire you, and they can help motivate you. I wouldn't be where I am today without other people, and I'm not just talking about my audience, I'm talking about people who are competitors of mine who I've become friends with. I wish I knew how important that was because I tried to hide behind my keyboard. I tried to just write blog posts and feel like I don't have to talk to anybody because I was an introvert. I'm not somebody who goes out there and is naturally great at that kind of thing. I had to learn how to do it, and it took a lot of false starts, but it definitely helped me get to where I am today.

What are three pieces of software/technology you recommend people use in their business?

Calendar app in phone

Social media platform (Start with one to call home first.)

Podcasting platform

For somebody who has dreams of being a wildly successful entrepreneur with freedom, what is the most important thing to focus on?

The most important thing to focus on is, what does that actually mean to you? What does wildly successful mean to you? Wildly successful to one person is completely different to somebody else. All of your dreams coming true are your dreams, and unfortunately, we get so jaded by other people's dreams that we often take them as our own. That's one of the first things I talk about with a lot of people who I teach business to because that lays the foundation for the road map ahead and the

43

destination that we're going toward. The cool thing about that is when you know where you're going toward, you can take the right approach, and you can take the right exits. If you get off course, at least you can get back on course. Most people are flying around and losing energy, and all of a sudden, they're landing somewhere because they've overworked themselves or they're overwhelmed, and they might be further away from where they want to be.

Understanding clearly what your goals are. What does your day look like? Who are you with? What are you doing? I know a lot of people who are very successful on paper, but really, they're not happy at all, and the beauty of entrepreneurship—the beauty of being a creator—is you get to create whatever life you want. When you see somebody else's highlight reel and that's what you think you have to be or when my clients say they want to be a seven-figure entrepreneur and I ask them if that's a million dollars or nine million dollars, it's a completely different pathway. At the same time, do you really need a million dollars to live the happy life you want? It's funny because when we calculate it and go into the details, they realize, "Oh wow, I could do well with $150,000 a year." That's a completely different business model. That's a completely different set of things that you need to do. That's less customers you have to worry about. You can focus on less and serve them deeper. I know people making mid-six figures with just thirty clients, and that person is doing something different than if somebody wanted to create a hundred-million-dollar company or the next Tesla.

What is your definition of success?

For me, it's freedom of time to spend more time with my family or to dive into an interest that I might have. It's me knowing that I have this sort of squirrel syndrome where I get really interested in different things, so I want the time to be able to explore those things. Thus, the things that I have already said yes to, if and only if they are automated or there's a team or they're working on their own already, do I then allow myself to explore new things. For example, this year, I started a new YouTube channel because I now have the time to do that. We hired more team members, we have systems of automation in place, and now because I have an interest in Pokémon cards and collectibles and investing in that, I can dive deeply into that. I can get involved in that community. I can take all the experiences I had in my entrepreneurial space, in my entrepreneurial YouTube channel, and put it into this one.

This new channel has only been up for two weeks, and we've already passed one thousand subscribers because I've had the time to focus on it.

Most people never get started. What would you say to someone who has a dream but is holding back from making the plunge?

Number one, what is a consequence of you not getting started? Oftentimes, we think about the fact that we might fail, that there's fear, that we're procrastinating or have self-doubt, that maybe we aren't going to be good enough, that we have imposter syndrome, but most of the time what drives me forward to move on to new projects—and this is what I recommend to those who are just starting out—is asking, "What would happen if you didn't start? What would you feel when you are however many years old on your deathbed, regretting the idea of not starting?" That is pain, right there. You can't go back in time. You have time right now.

I remember a video that I saw of Gary Vaynerchuk, and there was a woman who rolled up in a car and saw Gary, and she asked if he had a piece of advice on how to stay motivated all the time and what he would say to everybody watching this. He goes into the camera, and he says, "You're gonna die." First of all, it hits you hard, and secondly, he explains that you're going to die one day so live every day to the fullest and make these decisions now because you're going to regret it completely if you don't.

I like to say I would much rather live a life full of "oh wells" than a life full of "what ifs." "Oh well, at least I gave it a shot" versus "what if that would have changed everything?" There is a quote from Les Brown that says, "The graveyard is the richest place on earth, because it is here that you will find all the hopes and dreams that were never fulfilled, the books that were never written, the songs that were never sung, the inventions that were never shared, the cures that were never discovered, all because someone was too afraid to take that first step, keep with the problem, or determined to carry out their dream."

Number two, start small and start on the things that actually matter for the business and helping people. That's really what it's all about: helping people. We often think we need one hundred customers. Well, what if you just get one? That narrows down your focus, the actions you need to take, and it will give you a nice test of validation, not just that you can do this and help people, but whether or not you even want to go down that route.

Why commit to one hundred? Get that first customer. It's going to teach you so much. Just find one and help them, and then focus on the thing you need to do instead of making a website, creating a logo, or getting business cards. That stuff feels good. It feels like the sexy thing to do because it makes it seem like a real business now, but it's actually not. You're procrastinating from what the business actually is. Find the one client. If you, for example, are a singer, and you want to get people to take singing lessons from you, you don't have to have your whole calendar filled out yet. You don't even have to know how you're going to accept payments. Just find one person who will say yes to getting a lesson from you and just start there, and even if you do it for free just to get experience and a testimonial, great. Start with the network that you have, and while these people might not be people who want to learn how to sing, they are your advocates.

When they see that you put yourself out there and share that you are looking to help people learn to sing and you are willing to do it for cheap because you are experimenting and learning how to do this, they're going to go to bat for you if you've gone to bat for them. This takes us to the final lesson here, which is the idea of digging your well before you're thirsty, and this goes back to what we talked about with relationships. If the moment you ask somebody or if the moment you reach out to somebody for the first time is the moment you need something, it's too late. You haven't done the work to keep and uphold that relationship. You need to reach back out to people who are at the bottom of your message list and reconnect with them for no other reason than to just reconnect with them. That's you digging your well now before you're thirsty because there might come a point where maybe you have a business idea or maybe something happens like you get laid off and you need some support, and those are the people who are going to come to bat for you because you've kept that connection and you're not just asking them for stuff out of nowhere.

How do you relentlessly pursue excellence, greatness, and success (however you define it), while at the same time enjoy the journey of life?

It's being conscious about what you're doing and what's happening. I think a lot of us get into robot mode or workhorse mode, and we just kind of go, go, go, and life is just passing by. I had to slow down, be present, and appreciate and be grateful for things, which is actually one thing that I do every single day. I wake up in the morning and I write in my Five-Minute Journal what the three things I'm most grateful for are. It changes every day, and there are a lot of repeats, but it allows me to start the day with positivity. Then I write down the three things that I really want to achieve during the day. At the end of the day, I go back into the journal and there's a spot to write down three great, amazing things that have happened from the day, and I continue that momentum moving forward.

When I have the yearly plan and the five-year plan, and I understand what my vision is and where I want to go, that can then help me think about things like what was my day like today and where I am now in relation to that. Am I making progress towards that goal? I can have the perfect combination of long-term vision and short-term working cohesively.

What is one action you recommend someone do every day to be the best version of themselves?

I think that meditation has actually been huge for me, especially in this day and age where things are happening so fast and everything is racing and I have so many ideas. Even just taking three minutes to take a breath, calm down, turn on your HeadSpace app or some other thing to help you meditate can make an impact. I thought it was the silliest thing in the world when I first heard about meditation and how it can help a person develop as a creative, as an entrepreneur, as a human. I thought it was that I had to be at a Buddhist temple sitting with my fingers touching and sort of humming and have a very clear mind, and that's not what it's about. People like Tim Ferriss, Tony Robbins, and many other high performers meditate because having the ability to have a focused mind is really something that feeds into everything else that you do.

Here's the other byproduct of meditation that's been really key. Now that I've been practicing meditation, when I get distracted during the day, it's so easy for me to get back on track. So often we waste hours in the day moving from one task to the other. Getting into the flow state is so key because otherwise, that's hours in the day that you're potentially wasting by being distracted or changing tasks. Of course, we can't control all the things that are happening that might distract us, but we can control how quickly we get back into things.

How have relationships—personal and professional— contributed to your success and happiness?

They're everything. I wouldn't be here today without them. In relation to happiness in general, I think we as a species are a community-centric being, and we want to connect and feel a sense of belonging. That's really what it comes down to. As somebody who has actively gone out to seek communities that I could be a part of, and also somebody who's also created communities where people can find each other, it provides the motivation, the connections, the inspiration, the random happenstance interactions that can turn into something else. You never know when you put two separate people in a room together, what beautiful thing might come out of that. I think, especially with the tools that we have access to today, we have the ability to really amplify opportunities to connect. Unfortunately, a lot of us feel like these tools are actually separating us a little bit more, and I think that it depends on how you use them. My personal life has been incredible because of the things I've learned in business, and my business life has been incredible because of the things I've learned personally and from my wife, in particular. Once you start to build even just a small Rolodex, it's not that hard to find the things or the people you need to help you, but again, if you can help others first, it becomes much, much easier.

Who are three of your favorite entrepreneurs to follow, learn from, and/or connect with?

Elon Musk

Benjamin Franklin

Mark Rober

ALEXI PANOS

Bio

A leader in the Emergent Wisdom movement, Alexi Panos was named one of *Forbes'* Top 11 Women Entrepreneurs, *Inc.* magazine's Top 10 Entrepreneurs Changing the World, and *Origin* magazine's Top 100 Creatives Changing the World. She is a featured expert in the films, *The Abundance Factor, Rise Up,* and *Age of the Entrepreneur.* Alexi is a Master Leadership and Embodiment trainer in The Bridge Method workshops and The Elementum Coaching Institute (which she co-founded and developed with her husband Preston Smiles), and she hosts *Unleashed,* a podcast ranked as one of the top ten self-improvement podcasts. Alexi is a business strategist, artist, and humanitarian (through her organizations EPIC and The Sisters Society). As a best-selling author, Alexi has authored the books *50 Ways to Yay!* and *Now or Never,* both published by Simon & Schuster.

How to Connect

IG: @alexipanos

YT: /alexipanos

Website: alexipanos.com

How We Met

Alexi was someone a friend recommended I check out. I immediately liked what I saw and was introduced to her. Fast forward a few weeks, and the interview was scheduled and in the books.

What is the one thing that, if you knew when starting, would have accelerated your path to success?

You cannot fail. You cannot fail, so stop letting fear dictate your decisions and stop letting your current paradigm dictate what you're going after because you can't fail. Every step you take will open up new possibilities and new paradigms of what's next, so take that step with confidence and know you'll get exactly what you need.

What are three pieces of software/technology you recommend people use in their business?

Google Drive

Voice Memos

Zoom

For somebody who has dreams of being a wildly successful entrepreneur with freedom, what is the most important thing to focus on?

You have to start with where you're at and what you have. I think everybody's trying to skip to chapter ten without doing chapters one through nine, and what they don't get is no matter where you're at, you have something valuable to offer. You may not be valuable to someone like Elon Musk, but you're valuable to somebody who's ten steps behind you. If you can provide some sort of value to them, whether it's a product or a service or a level of expertise, you're crushing it. And no matter where you're at, you are ten steps ahead of somebody else. I think we often mistake where we're at, especially when we're comparing ourselves to the Elon Musks of the world, and we think, "Who am I, and what do I have to offer the world?" There are so many people doing amazing things, but there's somebody looking at you saying the same thing. We have to humble ourselves and remind ourselves that where we are today is ten steps ahead of where we were five, ten, twenty years ago. That is where we start.

No entrepreneurial journey goes from A to B in a straight line. How did you overcome the internal doubts and external adversity along the journey?

I don't necessarily see external adversity. I know I've had a lot, and I've had some crazy stuff happen, but I truly have reframed any challenges as opportunities. I look at it as an opportunity, so any time I'm in my business where I'm faced with "how do I cross this line," "how do I up level past this upper limit," "how do I break through this threshold that I've been under for the last six years," I see it as opportunity. I tell myself the answer exists; it's here, I just don't have the paradigm for it. I just don't have the awareness of it yet, so how can I start thinking outside of my current paradigm, my current understanding, and come up with some creative solutions that could be the answer to that? It allows me to really face it with this level of curiosity and play. I consider myself a creative being. I love my creative faculties, and I use them all the time, so whenever I'm able to use them in that way, I'm like, "Yes, let's do this. Let's see what I'm made of. Let's see what I got." It becomes so fun. I face all the ups and downs and the lefts and rights and all the crazy twists and turns along the way with a level of enthusiasm, and I think that's what leads to my success—how I relate to it.

What is your definition of success?

It changes all the time, but currently it's being present to the magic of life and saying yes to my highest expression in the moment.

How do you relentlessly pursue excellence, greatness, and success (however you define it), while at the same time enjoy the journey of life?

The beautiful thing about that definition of success is it is about enjoying the journey. I've had a lot of learning in putting success outside of myself, putting success as a metric in my bank account, putting it as a metric in what I own or can acquire, and I got a lot of stuff. I got a lot of money, a lot of significance, a lot of notoriety, and none of that feels any different. I've been really blessed along the way to have that at a young age because I had success in a bunch of different industries. So, for me, I had that lesson multiple times until I was like, "Wait a second, this external pursuit really doesn't mean anything, so when are you going to get it and actually shift?" Even though society says it's out here, just shift

51

it to in here, and the minute I did that, I was winning every day. My life was a success because I'm choosing to be present in life, and life includes all of it—the ups and downs, the good, the bad, all of it. If I can be present to that and say yes to my highest expression in the face of it, then you can't lose.

What is one action you recommend someone do every day to be the best version of themselves?

I think rituals are different for everybody because everybody taps in differently, but I would say the one thing that could serve everyone is stillness and silence.

I don't mean like go meditate, but stillness and silence. I don't love meditating and sitting down and putting time aside for that ritual. However, I love giving myself moments of silence and stillness in nature, sitting by the water, walking through the forest, or just sitting under a tree and watching the tree teach me based on its lessons in its nature. There's so much magic in the space between, and we don't give ourselves opportunities for that because we're so busy, and there are so many things to do and so many people to serve and so many emails to answer. So, when we just stop, we get out of that habitual pattern of who we are, and we get clear on who we *actually* are.

How have relationships—personal and professional—contributed to your success and happiness?

Relationships are the greatest transformation that you could possibly step into. I lead workshops that are super intense, and people walk into these rooms, and they leave changed. They say it was the hardest thing they've ever done, but they feel so incredible. I always joke and say, "You think that's hard? Try being a parent, try being intimate, and try being seen on a level that's not just surface." That's the most incredible opportunity for transformation. It's been the most powerful mirror for all the places that I wasn't willing to show up for myself yet, for all the places where I was inauthentic, for all the places where I was hiding out, for all the places where I was triggered, and all those triggers represented parts of myself that I was unwilling to accept or look at or express. So, it's been everything. I can do all the personal development work on myself, but until it's tested in the trenches of relationships, it means nothing.

Who are three of your favorite entrepreneurs to follow, learn from, and/or connect with?

Jill Stanton: She's a soul sister, a badass biz woman, dreams and plays big, moms and wifes with fun and flow!

Richard Branson: An oldie but goodie. He's always inspired me to keep dreaming big and paving paths that don't yet exist. Have fun, give back, make life matter, and do it unapologetically!

Elon Musk: Dreams super big dreams and really considers the impact of the choices he makes.

HOW TO HANDLE REJECTION AS AN ENTREPRENEUR

When I am working with entrepreneurs, one of the most common fears I hear is *rejection.*

Why haven't you started? Rejection. I don't want to start something and then people not accept me for going after my dreams.

Why haven't you reached out to any prospects yet? Rejection. I don't want to annoy someone. I don't want to reach out and have them tell me no.

Why haven't you asked for help? Rejection. I don't want to open myself up only to be told no.

Why haven't you reached out to someone you look up to? Rejection. I don't want to risk them not talking to me.

I hate to break it to you, but here's the truth . . .

You *will* be rejected on your path to becoming an Elevated Entrepreneur!

I've never met someone who went from start to star without facing rejection.

Every single person I interviewed in this book has been rejected. The crazy thing is, more often than not, rejection is a catalyst to their success.

For this book alone, I must have been rejected more than one hundred times. I was rejected by people who didn't want to participate. I was rejected by people who wouldn't make introductions. I was rejected by people who wouldn't help me in the development of this book.

Does it mean this idea isn't good? No.

Does it mean they didn't like the idea? No.

Does it mean I am any less of a human being? No.

Maybe it was the wrong time.

Maybe it wasn't the right fit.

Maybe their schedule was already booked.

Maybe they wanted to let others have the opportunity.

The thing we have to remember is, when someone says no, it is not a reflection on you as a human being.

So, let's spend a minute here reframing the dreaded *no*.

No stands for New Opportunity.

No doesn't mean it's over or never going to happen. It just means not yet.

No can be used as fuel to ignite the fire within you to keep persevering.

Every no you face gets you closer to a yes.

No gives you a chance to improve and reflect.

No is an opportunity to find someone or something better.

Instead of seeing no as this two-letter word that has immense control over us, let's reframe it and see it for what it is.

The fact is, hearing no is inevitable, but what you do when you hear no can be the difference in you succeeding and giving up.

STU MCLAREN

Bio

Stu McLaren coaches and consults New York Times best-selling authors, top-rated speakers, experts, and niche celebrities on how to launch, grow, and scale high-profit, recurring revenue streams.

As the former founder of the world's #1 membership platform for WordPress, WishList Member, he had the chance to serve and support over 60,000 online communities and membership sites. Through that experience, he gained a unique insight into the subtle membership nuances that produce massive results.

Today, he uses that knowledge to help his clients launch and grow multiple high six-and seven-figure membership sites, and he shares the same blueprints at membershipworkshop.com.

How to Connect
IG: @stumclaren
Website: stu.me

How We Met

Stu is an industry legend for online entrepreneurs. I had been hearing his name all over the place, so I shot him a DM and told him how pumped I was to meet him and how everyone always spoke so highly of him. Shortly after, I realized he is a huge Toronto Raptors fan, so I got him and his son tickets to an NBA playoff game as virtual fans. A few months later, I invited him to be part of this book. Between our schedules, it took four follow-ups before we officially had a date on the calendar, but it was 100% worth it.

What is the one thing that, if you knew when starting, would have accelerated your path to success?

I think I would have given myself a lot of grace in the beginning because I think in the beginning, it's about figuring stuff out, and to figure stuff out, you have to start trying stuff. Too often I see people get stuck trying to think of the perfect idea, and they're waiting and waiting and waiting. The reality of it is, you get clarity from doing stuff. You get clarity from taking action. If I look at where I'm at now, I would never have guessed that I would be helping people generate recurring revenue, that I'd be training people, or that I'd have a software company. I would never have thought that, but the way in which I got here was through a series of doing stuff, trying stuff, and it leads one step closer to where you eventually want to be, so I think that's what I would have said to myself earlier. Give yourself some grace, try things in the beginning, and be open-minded to the fact that this is a long game. I was trying to come up with the perfect idea, especially in the early days, instead of just giving myself that grace and just trying things.

What are three pieces of software/technology you recommend people use in their business?

Searchie.io

StreamYard

Airtable

For somebody who has dreams of being a wildly successful entrepreneur with freedom, what is the most important thing to focus on?

One of the things that I really want to encourage people who are in the early stages is to really pay attention because what we ultimately want to center on is becoming known for something specific. You want to become known for solving a specific problem.

For a long time, I was trying to help all entrepreneurs with all things marketing, and it was a really tough uphill battle because I wasn't known for anything specific, so people didn't really know how to refer me, and they didn't really know how to send me business, so I felt like I was pushing a boulder up a hill. Then one day, a friend and mentor of mine,

Reid Tracy, who's the CEO of the big publishing company called Hay House, Inc. asked me why I wasn't just focused on helping people create memberships since that's what I'd been doing for decades. To be honest, my ego was just like no, but he's infinitely more wise and has so much more experience than me, and so I decided to try it out. I started leaning into the fact that this was my area of expertise—which it had been for years—I just hadn't owned it, and the crazy thing was, the moment that I started leaning into the fact that this is my area of expertise, all kinds of doors started opening up. People knew exactly who to refer to me because if they had a problem with the membership site: if it had flatlined, if they wanted to launch the membership, it was "Go see Stu." Anything related to membership sites, it was "Go see Stu" because I became known for solving a specific problem. So, if you want to experience more traction faster than ever before, become known for solving a specific problem.

The perfect analogy is to think about a doctor. Let's say you've got a knee problem. We're big basketball fans, so imagine Fred Van Fleet goes down with a knee injury. Who is he going to want to go see? Is he going to want to go see a general doctor or is he going to want to go see the best knee specialist he can? He's going to go see the best knee specialist he can, and he's going to pay a premium to see that person because they specialize in that one thing. As early entrepreneurs, we get scared that if we specialize, we're closing ourselves off to the rest of the world, and I'm here to tell you, no, you're not. The reality of it is if you focus your front-end messaging on solving one specific problem, you're going to end up welcoming so many more people so much faster, and then once they're in your world, you can open them up to the rest of the things that you do, but in the beginning, focus your front-end messaging on solving one specific problem, and by golly, you'll grow faster than you can imagine.

What is your definition of success?

I would really define it in two areas. There's personal success, and then there's business success. Personal success really boils down to a few key things. One, I want to really focus on having time for my most meaningful relationships, which is time with my kids, my wife, and my friends. Number two is I really want to make sure I use that time to create memories. I just read a book recently called *Die with Zero,* and the essence of the book is that so many people build so much wealth and then they get to the years when they're "retired," and then they're really too old to be able to enjoy that wealth. All the things they would have loved to have done in their prime years like going on ski trips or adventures, they just can't do anymore, so they sit there with all this wealth that they can't ever really use, and the whole book is about using the money that you make during your peak years, so to speak, where you can really enjoy it, and so we are all about creating memories as a family.

Then the other thing when it comes to the personal side is having impact and impact means different things to different people. For my wife and me, it means impacting our family and friends, our local community, those that we serve, and impacting the world. I'll give you one example. I love making money because money is just a resource that enables us to do more cool things for more cool people. If you're a good-hearted person and you have more money, it means you could do more cool stuff and you can have more impact. One of the things that my wife and I do on a personal level is each year we create a Super Surprise. We pick a loved one, a friend or family member, who we create an experience for that will be an experience of a lifetime that they would never be able to do for themselves, and it creates this amazing memory together, and it deepens the relationship. That's all possible because of what we do on the business side.

Now, on the business side, business is an incredible opportunity to be able to make a whole lot of money because as an entrepreneur, there are no limits. There are no limits on how much you can make or how much I can make. When we're in a job, there's limits. There are limits on your salary, the number of days of vacation, on what you can and can't wear, and all these other things. To heck with that. I got into entrepreneurship for that freedom to be able to do the things that I love and not be restricted.

When my wife took me to Kenya for the very first time, and we were looking to build our first school for our non-profit called Village Impact where we build schools in rural areas of Kenya, I was talking to the chairman of this community, and I was trying to find out how much things cost. We had no experience building schools, so I asked him how much it costs to fund the full-time salary of a teacher. He thought for a moment, and he said it's about one hundred dollars a month. At that moment, a light bulb went off. At the time, I was selling a piece of software, and it was selling for one hundred dollars a license, and I thought that if I sell one more license a month, and I just allocate that to funding the full-time salary of a teacher, imagine the impact I could have. Then the real lightbulb went off, which was "What if I make a whole lot more money?" That would mean I could allocate a whole lot more to the people and causes that I'm passionate about.

That's when I started to get really excited about business because I realized in that moment, the more money I make, the more impact I can have. For a long time, I struggled with making a lot of money because in mid to late twenties, I was making more money than both my parents combined, and I felt guilty about it. Inevitably, my subconscious would kick in at different times, and it would be like, "Whoa, Stu. You're from a blue-collar family. This is too much." And then I would stop doing the things that had made me a success. But that moment in Kenya, everything clicked and changed. It helped me realize money is a really good thing, and thank goodness that we are in a position where we own our own business and there are no limits because when we've got more money, we can do more good. That's why I love being an entrepreneur, and for me, making a whole lot of money is the focus because with a whole lot of money, we can do a whole lot of good.

One of the things that I love about the market that we help is because we help so many entrepreneurs in so many different markets generate recurring revenue, when I speak to them about the impact they can have with business, it has that ripple effect. At the end of the day, the thing that we obsess about in our business is helping people generate more recurring revenue. We obsess over it, and we obsess over the stories of the people that we serve because we know that's going to have an extended ripple to the people that they serve, and so ultimately, we're impacting millions and millions of people. The beautiful part about it is that everybody wins. They win because they grow and generate more recurring revenue, and we win because it helps grow our business, and the people that we then get to help with the income that we make win as well. Hopefully, that gives an overview on the personal side and on the business side.

How do you relentlessly pursue excellence, greatness, and success (however you define it), while at the same time enjoy the journey of life?

I'm held accountable 100% by my two kids and my wife. They keep me accountable to enjoy life, especially my wife. She's really been the one that has opened me up to experiences. Truth be told, if I didn't have my wife, who is constantly encouraging and helping organize that side of things, I'd probably be a hermit. I'd be the guy stuck in my own little world, not going out anywhere, maybe going outside for a run, but she's the one that's really helped me create the memories, and I'm so grateful to her for that.

At the end of the day, this is what we do. We map out our year and the big rocks that go on the calendar are the experiences that we want to have as a family. They go on the calendar first, and then everything else gets sprinkled around those. This is why we do what we do, to have these experiences as a family, to create these memories as a family, and that's why they go in the calendar first.

What is one action you recommend someone do every day to be the best version of themselves?

I can't say what's going to be best for everybody because everybody is going to be different, but I can tell you what's best for me. The one action that I do every day is I start and end the day with my family. I wish I could say that I have some big fancy morning routine, but I have two young kids. My routine means waking up to my son who's six inches from my face with morning breath, asking if I can help him get breakfast. When I start my day with the kids in the morning, I'm up and getting them breakfast. During that time, we're having conversations, we're connecting.

Then similarly, we end the day together. Every night, we have dinner as a family. We are either going for a walk as a family, playing board games as a family, or we're doing something as a family, but we have a very set routine in the evening where we're together. When I think about keeping priorities front and center, that's what's worked for us, and that's what's worked for me.

How have relationships—personal and professional— contributed to your success and happiness?

Relationships are everything. At the end of the day, you can take everything away from me and I could start from zero and I'd be able to hit the reset button and get back to where I am fairly quickly because of the relationships. I think we have to realize relationships are an investment. It's not something that you take from when you need it; it's something that you continuously invest in. I'll give you a great little daily practice. One of the things that I have done is I've made a big list with hundreds and hundreds of names on an Airtable, and every day, I reach out to five of those people. It's just a quick simple text like, "Hey, what's going on in your world? What has you excited? Let me know." Whether it's a text, an Instagram direct message, or whatever, inevitably, it gets conversations started, and it allows you to connect with people. I'm intentional about going through the list so that I connect with everybody on that list at least once a quarter, because life changes and there's all kinds of things happening, but inevitably what happens is it continues to deepen the relationship.

You learn about people, and you learn what's going on in the world. In some sense, some of my friends in the past year experienced their biggest year ever by a landslide. In another sense, I have friends of mine who own brick and mortar retail shops and restaurants and breweries who suffered big time and have been scrambling and have hit a really hard time. You just never know what's going on in people's lives.

I think at the end of the day, relationships—both personal and professional—are so critical and important, but you have to remember to invest in them. You can't take, take, take from them. You have to invest in them. What ends up happening is when you do have an ask, people show up in spades and they are more than happy to help. When I think about our charity and what we've been able to do in building fourteen schools educating more than five thousand kids a day, I'm so grateful. That wouldn't be possible if it weren't for the relationships that we have built over the years. When it comes to relationships, play the long game, invest in them, and what'll end up happening is that people will show up in ways that you can't even begin to imagine.

Who are three of your favorite entrepreneurs to follow, learn from, and/or connect with?

Russell Brunson

The Secret Billionaire Mystery Man

Sara Blakely

STEVE O'DELL

Bio

CEO and co-founder at Tenzo, an omni-channel matcha brand. UCLA dropout.

How to Connect

IG: @sodellicious

LI: /sodellicious

TW: @sodell244

How We Met

Steve and I met in a Sunday basketball league with a bunch of entrepreneurs. We hit it off with John Stockton–Karl Malone chemistry and quickly grew our friendship. Within months, we became great friends, and shortly after, I became an investor in Tenzo. Fast forward a few years, and we continue to lift each other up and support each other the best we can.

What is the one thing that, if you knew when starting, would have accelerated your path to success?

To give a quick background, I dropped out of UCLA having never taken a business course in my life, so I would say understanding finance is the number one thing that I would have learned earlier. Managing cash flow, inventory, and then projecting that out would have been my focus. We went about two years without having a very good financial model, and those two years were rocky.

What are three pieces of software/technology you recommend people use in their business?

Notion

Shopify

Superhuman

Zapier

For somebody who has dreams of being a wildly successful entrepreneur with freedom, what is the most important thing to focus on?

If you want to be wildly successful, I think that backs into this concept of growth. You need to grow your company, and that is a very challenging thing because it's very different to get your first customer than it is to get your first one hundred customers than it is to get your first ten thousand, and so on. As the business changes, you need to adapt personally. If your personal growth does not match the company's growth, there's this common mental model, The Peter Principal, which means you basically get stuck at your highest level of competence. If you want to be a widely successful entrepreneur, I would focus on learning and growing your business.

No entrepreneurial journey goes from A to B in a straight line. How did you overcome the internal doubts and external adversity along the journey?

At a macro level, I think it's about managing mental health. It's about gratitude, journaling, talking to your family, and having good friends. Even just some of the conversations we, as good friends, have are super important. Keep a good head on your shoulders and have good friends and family.

What is your definition of success?

It's different for personal versus the company. The company has refined goals called OKRs (objectives and key results) that we need to hit over a period of time. Personally, I want to be happy every day. I love what I do. It's super fulfilling, and I'm surrounded by beautiful people that are inspiring and do a lot of good for the world, so I want to wake up and be happy every day. And I think if I do that, then that is success in itself.

Most people never get started. What would you say to someone who has a dream but is holding back from making the plunge?

Depending on where you are in life, if you have kids and a family to support, it might be a little different, but for everyone who is young and gunning or by themselves and has a little bit of savings, I would say burn the ships. Get started on something new, and then cut off all your means for safety, and figure it out. That can be perceived as really risky, but I think it's fine, and I think you will literally force yourself to be successful. You can be flexible in your approach as it's not a straight shot, but be really rigid in your goal.

How do you relentlessly pursue excellence, greatness, and success (however you define it), while at the same time enjoy the journey of life?

I actually consider this two different types of learning. One is domain learning, which is that I need to be a great CEO right now. We have objectives that we need to hit, so how do I figure out what those are and then hit them? The second one is how do I see that larger picture? I think with the internet and books, you can literally read almost everything about other successful people, so I spend a lot of time diving into their journeys and the lessons they learned at each stage to help me get prepared and to match my ambition.

What is one action you recommend someone do every day to be the best version of themselves?

I think there's five, and it's so funny because everyone talks about them, but not everyone is committed. I would say I get a decent amount of sleep every night. Wake up and have a sound morning routine. Journal and meditate throughout the day. Be really focused on your to-do list. At night, set time to do things and unwind, whether that's going out to dinner with friends or having a good conversation with your significant other.

How have relationships—personal and professional—contributed to your success and happiness?

They are critical. I'm the type of guy where I do not associate with people that I feel like will bring me down or are negative or judgmental or envious or all of those things. I want to be surrounded by this tribe of people that are on the same ship, and they're going for big things, and they're changing the world. Professionally, we have a really good group of friends, and everyone is on the same boat. Personally, I think it's about really good, sound, long-term relationships. I still keep really close contact with all my family. I call my dad almost every single day. I still have my best friends from childhood, and we're in the same group-chat shooting the shit every day. It's a good balance, and they help bring me back to reality sometimes because I feel everyone's out here making a million dollars or raising a ton of money, and you can get caught up in this fantasy land. People have real jobs and real issues too, so it's a good leveler.

Who are three of your favorite entrepreneurs to follow, learn from, and/or connect with?

Elon Musk

Brandin Cohen

Robbie Page

JORDAN YOUNGER

Bio

Jordan Younger is the blogger and spiritual teacher behind the top read wellness and lifestyle blog, *The Balanced Blonde,* as well as the host of *Forbes'* acclaimed podcast *SOUL ON FIRE,* where real conversations meet wellness, spirituality, high vibes, and awakening. Jordan is also an author, intuitive recipe developer, and the creator of The Balanced Blonde digital store filled with her high vibrational offerings. She lives in Los Angeles with her beautiful family and can be found wandering the aisles of Erewhon any day of the week!

How to Connect

IG: @thebalancedblonde

Website: thebalancedblonde.com

How We Met

Jordan is someone who I've seen time and time again but had never spoken with. When her name was brought up as someone who would be a great interview for this book, I looked around and found someone who could introduce me to her. We ended up having a lot of friends in common, so making this interview happen was a no brainer.

What is the one thing that, if you knew when starting, would have accelerated your path to success?

I started my blogging business in such a different way than most people do. I pretty much fell into the career of blogging. I was blogging for fun before it was ever an option to be a career! I started it naturally, and after about a year, it took off to the point where I decided to leave grad school to pursue the blog full-time. I am happy with the way I did it, and I don't think I could have done anything differently because the industry was so brand-new. It was basically the wild west! I know in my heart that everything happened the way it was supposed to. But if I could think of one thing I would have done differently, I wouldn't have said yes to so many opportunities. I said yes to *everything*. Now, with the foresight that I have, I would have held off on a lot of things in the beginning. I don't necessarily align with everything I did a decade ago! I did so much of saying yes for the first four to five years before I realized there's such a power and such a magic in waiting for the right opportunities. In letting go of certain things, even if they seem so glamorous, even if they're so lucrative, even if they're going to make you more "famous" or give you more of a status, it's not always all that it's cracked up to be. So, I'm just much pickier, much choosier with everything that I do and everything that I say yes to now!

What are three pieces of software/technology you recommend people use in their business?

GarageBand

WordPress

Slack

For somebody who has dreams of being a wildly successful entrepreneur with freedom, what is the most important thing to focus on?

I think it's so important to focus on doing what you really love. In the beginning, you might be the only person at your company, so you have to love it because you're going to end up working a lot. I don't want to say you will work 24/7, but definitely every day in the week. There are not going to be standard hours, and there's not going to be anyone else telling you to get it done, so you have to love it. I have seen so many people start something and then crash and burn because of the time and the effort and the energy that it requires, but if you love your subject matter and you're truly inspired and lit up by what you're doing, then you'll take it all the way. It might not happen overnight, but I do believe that all the most wildly successful people that I know are so lit up by what they're doing and so passionate about their subject and brand. You don't have to be afraid to change, so if you start something and you realize "maybe I'm not passionate about this anymore," just pivot and change.

I have done so many things within the umbrella of The Balanced Blonde. I actually started as The Blonde Vegan and then transitioned to being The Balanced Blonde within a year. Then I pivoted over a hundred times, it felt like. I was a full-time yoga blogger/yoga teacher for many years. I don't talk too much about fitness or yoga anymore, not because I don't love it, but because my own journey has gone so much deeper, and I'm so interested in talking about the things that are a little bit more out there, so also know that if your interests are not mainstream, there's always an audience for what you're talking about.

What is your definition of success?

I think that in order to be successful, you have to be happy with what you're waking up to and doing every day, and you also have to never lose yourself in the process. I've been guilty of this by becoming my brand identity and becoming the way everyone else sees me, so I had to get back to who I am in my heart in order to feel successful and happy. I think success is going through life enjoying what you're doing and enjoying waking up every day, and that's not something that everybody gets to experience. In fact, it's something a lot of people don't get to experience, but I want to help people see that it's possible, and it's possible for everyone.

We live in a world where we can all be the creators of our own destiny, so never forget that because that is the ultimate success. And then, of course, when we're recognized for doing that. When we have customers or we have an audience, I think that's the ultimate success because it means what you're doing and what you're creating is really resonating with people.

What is one action you recommend someone do every day to be the best version of themselves?

I would recommend being alone with yourself every day whether that's meditating, journaling, or going on a walk outside in quietude and truly being alone with your own thoughts because that's when we can be creative and that's when we can tap into really acting versus reacting.

How have relationships—personal and professional—contributed to your success and happiness?

In every way. In my twenties, I worked so much that I put work before people at times, and then I realized that is a very lonely existence to the point where at the end of the day, when you launch something exciting, you want to celebrate it with the people in your life, so the people in my life are first and foremost. Also, the people in my life are the ones who introduce me to the coolest people that I've met that have enhanced my own life. I think life is all about connections and people and having beautiful experiences with people that we love.

Who are three of your favorite entrepreneurs to follow, learn from, and/or connect with?

Brandin Cohen

Gabby Bernstein

Glennon Doyle

JAY FERRUGGIA

Bio

Jay Ferruggia is a fitness expert, performance coach, speaker, author, and host of the Renegade Radio podcast, which has had millions of downloads since its launch in 2014. He's been a consultant and coach to professional athletes, Hollywood entertainers, and law enforcement and military personnel. And over the last two decades, he's helped more than 200,000 regular men make life-changing transformations. He's been featured in Men's Fitness, Men's Health, Muscle & Fitness, MMA Sports, Maximum Fitness, Details, Fast Company, Entrepreneur, The Huffington Post, CBS, and ESPN. He's also been named one of the Top 30 Health Influencers in the World.

How to Connect

IG: @jayferruggia

FB: /jayferruggia

TW: @jasonferruggia

Website: jasonferruggia.com

How We Met

I first heard about Jay through his podcast *Renegade Radio*. After knowing a few people on his show, I reached out to get to know him and pitch myself for his show. A couple of months later, I was on his show, and we started to become friends. As this book progressed, I asked Jay to be part of it because every time we chat, I leave fired up and excited for what's next! If I never reached out about his podcast, we might have never met. That's why it's so important to shoot your shot! Now, we're good friends and support each other the best we can.

What is the one thing that, if you knew when starting, would have accelerated your path to success?

I think my go-to on that would be the Bruce Lee concept of subtraction more than addition and simplifying. I was having this conversation at dinner with five colleagues the other night, and we were all saying that it always comes back to simplicity and focusing on the essentials. Take what's useful and reject what's not. Try not to get caught up in all the new things or in shiny-object syndrome. Also, when you're working with any kind of client on any transformation, know that they don't need everything. As a coach, you might have a million things in your toolbox, but they only need three of them, and then they need those three things repeated fifty-two weeks a year for a decade straight.

For somebody who has dreams of being a wildly successful entrepreneur with freedom, what is the most important thing to focus on?

I think the most important thing for an entrepreneur is to get up and own your morning and have five daily non-negotiables. Create non-negotiables that you can adhere to each day. Own your morning. Read that book. Don't start the morning reactively; start it proactively. That means get up, do something for me, stretch, exercise, whatever. And then once you're doing that, you can figure out the rest.

A lot of times, we hear people say they want to leave their nine to five and start a side hustle, and the freedom is going to be so great. Then once they do it, the freedom is the worst thing ever because they don't know what they're doing, and now they're working twenty hours a day. So, you really need to create structure and discipline. I think that's probably the most important thing, more so than any kind of specific tactics or building funnels. Create that structure. It's a cliché, but you have to take care of yourself first. If the plane is going down, put your mask on first.

What is your definition of success?

Success to me is making enough money that I could help the people that I care about and spend time with them without having to work eighteen hours a day. I don't want to quadruple my income if it means I have to work eighteen hours a day. I want to spend time with people. Life is all about experiences. I would say spending time with people that I love and having the freedom financially to do it.

Most people never get started. What would you say to someone who has a dream but is holding back from making the plunge?

For anyone trying to start anything, make it super simple. Don't start The Rock's workout plan or The Rock's diet, and don't try to become Mark Cuban in business tomorrow. What's one simple thing you can do? I tell most people, if they're training, don't even get a gym membership. Let's just get you doing push-ups and bodyweight squats for ten minutes. Can we do that once a day? Three times a week? Then let's build that habit. Now, let's add a little bit more to that, and maybe then we'll buy some stuff for the home gym or get you a gym membership. If you're going to start a business, it has to be really simple. Just start something.

Also, you have to get over the fear of people judging you. That's really the main reason that people don't take risks and do a lot of things: because they're worried their family is going to judge them or some random on the internet will judge them. You have to get over that. That's in your head. The reality is, even though we think that the world is full of haters and things like that, most people want you to succeed, and if you do succeed, good people will always be happy for you. I think we need to get over that false narrative that people want you to fail and that everyone can't wait to make fun of you and cancel you and things like that. That's not really true. People do want you to succeed.

How do you relentlessly pursue excellence, greatness, and success (however you define it), while at the same time enjoy the journey of life?

It's always a balance. I think it's in my East Coast DNA to hustle, and I could hustle nonstop and out-work anyone, but I'll also out-party anyone, and I'll also have a better social life. That's the greatest compliment to me. When friends of mine who are multimillionaires, like Bedros Keuilian or somebody like that says, "You have more fun than anybody I know, and you have a bigger social circle than anybody I know." There's a lot of guys who are multimillionaires, but you can't talk to them about anything but business, and these guys are like, "I don't know anyone who's more into music than you," or "I don't anyone who knows more about pro wrestling than you do." I have a pretty good balance. It's always a challenge, but I go all in. People who know me well will tell you that I'm all in on everything all the time. Sometimes, I get a little burned out from that, but that's why I take care of myself. Every single week, I'm in the sauna multiple times, in float tanks, getting a massage multiple times a week, getting dry needling, paddle boarding out on the lake, or hiking. I go hard all the time, but then I have the balance of that other stuff, and I go hard on the recovery stuff too.

What is one action you recommend someone do every day to be the best version of themselves?

I would say exercise. I think physical fitness is still the foundation, for sure. That's number one.

How have relationships—personal and professional— contributed to your success and happiness?

Every single way possible. For more than thirty years, I didn't have a lot of close friends. I had a lot of people that I was around, and we would hang out but nothing like I do now. When I moved to LA eleven years ago, my priority was to really build relationships. I read a lot of books on it and figured all this stuff out. In terms of business, I would not be anywhere near where I am without the relationships that I built and without friends and mentors to support me. I have the most amazing inner circle of people that I can always lean on and go to, so I think relationships just open countless doors for you.

Now, I don't have anyone in my circle who doesn't lift me up, who doesn't make me better, who doesn't make me laugh, who talks shit, who gossips. So, any time I get with those people, it's like I just had ten cups of coffee, and my energy is through the roof. I'm sitting there, and I can't believe these people are my friends. I can't believe this is my life. This is amazing. It's everything. So, if people are struggling with that, and I was, I would tell you that you have to read How to Win Friends and Influence People.

Who are three of your favorite entrepreneurs to follow, learn from, and/or connect with?

Bedros Keuilian

Dwayne "The Rock" Johnson

Joe Rogan

Seth Godin

ALISON J. PRINCE

Bio

Alison J. Prince has built four lucrative multimillion-dollar online businesses from the ground up. She's been featured in *Forbes*, on the cover of *Costco Connection*, and has spoken on stages across the country.

She feels her most successful business choice was teaching her ten- and thirteen-year-old daughters how to sell over $100,000 in products in just nine months. She watched them gain confidence, embrace entrepreneurship, and begin to live what she terms the "Because I Can" life.

While continuing to run her companies, Alison is also committed to helping others achieve their financial goals. Through her successful $0–$100K System, she now teaches thousands how to create, launch, and grow profitable e-commerce businesses. Members of the Because I Can life appreciate her authentic, down-to-earth approach to business and life, along with her constant encouragement that they have the ability to do whatever they put their minds to. Why? Because They Can. Grab a free gift from Alison here: becauseicanlife.com/gift

How to Connect
IG: @alisonjprince
FB: /alisonjprince
Website: alisonjprince.com

How We Met

I read the book *30 Days* by Russell Brunson, which featured tons of entrepreneurs, and Alison was featured. I loved how she talked about parties and her strategy on what she would do if she had thirty days to start all over. I began following her, and as the guest list for this book kept growing, I asked a friend to make an intro. The intro was all we needed, and now we are quickly becoming good friends.

What is the one thing that, if you knew when starting, would have accelerated your path to success?

Listening to myself. I think the biggest thing we have issues with as entrepreneurs is when we go out there and we start asking the world, "What do you think about this product? What do you think about this idea?" We ask our friends and our family who absolutely love us and support us, but the dream that we were given was not given to them, and so they start to muddle it down, or they don't feel the excitement that we feel which starts to dilute it. Then, after we get feedback from all of them, we are so confused that we don't even know where to start.

I think that you know the dream. You know the step that you're supposed to take deep down inside of you, and you don't need to ask anybody. Just start. Those steps that I'm talking about are just little things. It's a half of a step, not even a sprint for ten miles down the road. I'm talking about just starting. Maybe it's your first Instagram post. Put it up there, and guess what? You're probably going to have zero followers, so you're going to get zero reaction. Perfect. I would much rather start at zero than start at a million when I bugger things up or I say the wrong things. I have to learn my voice before I can go forward. Or maybe it's selling a product. I'm in e-commerce, and I teach e-commerce a lot, so you don't have to sell your product to your friends or your family. There's plenty of places online you can sell, so quit listening to everybody else.

What are three pieces of software/technology you recommend people use in their business?

Google Docs

Trello

Lightroom

For somebody who has dreams of being a wildly successful entrepreneur with freedom, what is the most important thing to focus on?

The freedom. I talk to e-commerce people all the time, and they tell me they don't want to be stuck to a warehouse, and I tell them, "Then don't be stuck to a warehouse. Hire it out. Hire a fulfillment company to fulfill for you, so while you're sitting on the beach, you can hear the cha-chings going off on your phone knowing that your product is going to be shipped." I think sometimes we just get going and think "I have to do this; I have to do that." If freedom is the life that I want, it's asking, "Does this choice that's coming to me allow for freedom?" If it doesn't, don't choose it. There are always workarounds so that you can live the life that you choose to—that you want to.

What is your definition of success?

I think it's how it makes you feel. That's what I think success is. Success isn't money. Money is a resource, a renewable resource, and we can get it. The more value we put out in the world, the more money we can make.

It's knowing that your product, whatever you're selling, has the ability to impact a life. I think that's true success. It's the service. Service and serving your customers is the ultimate success. Money will come when we serve and when we put value out into the world.

How do you relentlessly pursue excellence, greatness, and success (however you define it), while at the same time enjoy the journey of life?

I think if you feel fulfilled, that helps you enjoy the journey. If you just go out there, and you sell crap or just sell stuff to sell stuff, it's not that inner fulfillment that makes you feel amazing. You don't feel that internal addiction of "oh, my gosh, I was able to impact someone else's life." It's easier for me to enjoy the journey because I remember the very first testimonial I got when I started going out online. I was so scared, and people were making fun of my eyebrows, but I remember I showed up for my people, and I said, "I'm here for you, let's do this," and their testimonials back were what kept me going even when I missed a sale or launched something that was a flub. It was the internal feeling of knowing that I was serving and showing up that kept me going and enjoying that success.

I've had my share of tears, believe me. I think we all have, but I think we have to have the dark and the frustration and the banging your head against the wall to be able to see the contrast, to see the opposites.

The house that we just moved into was painted orange. We called it the James and the Giant Peach, and I wasn't a fan of that. So now, it's getting painted this white, beautiful, bright color, and I love the contrast. I think as humans, we love contrast, and so when you're having that dark moment, know that this is going to be completely opposite. There is an opposite to what you are experiencing, and we can be grateful for when we see that, because if we didn't, we would never see it. We have to have that hard part to be able to experience the bright, the light, the joy, and the success in our businesses.

What is one action you recommend someone do every day to be the best version of themselves?

Remember your priorities. Humans first. Never sales first. For me, my first is my family, and I've structured it to where, when they were babies, I would get up at five o'clock in the morning and work until they woke up. Now that they're teenagers, they like to sleep in more, so I don't get up quite as early. When I get up now, I'm going to focus on them until they go to school, and they fill my heart and my soul. Then they go off to school and I'm 100% focused on business. When they come home from school, we play tennis, go shopping together, or go to the grocery store, but I get to be with them. The one thing is, remember the humans in your life. We do this for them, so don't get so distracted that you forget about what's really, really important.

How have relationships—personal and professional—contributed to your success and happiness?

They're everything. You literally cannot do this life alone. You literally cannot do business alone. We need the people of the grocery stores to get food for us. We need human beings to talk to us. We have to have humans in our life to even survive.

In business, when someone says they're just going to do it alone, I'm like, "No, no." Find businesspeople who are right where you're at, and then go find a few mentors to follow. Don't listen to all the mentors in the world because it'll spread you too thin; just choose a couple. Then find business friends who are in your sphere that can lift you up because your best friend doesn't know business and doesn't understand. When you make that first three dollars online and you are celebrating because you had to get through the head trash, you had to figure out technology, and you had to overcome so much stuff, and you're like, "I just made three dollars," they're going to come back to you and say you are a long way from making your first million. It's going to feel like they're a soul sucker, but if you go to a friend, they are going to celebrate the heck out of you because they knew what it took for you to get there. Find that tribe and find that community. Don't do business alone.

Who are three of your favorite entrepreneurs to follow, learn from, and/or connect with?

Russell Brunson

Cathy Heller

Jill Stanton

Greg McKeown

Benjamin Hardy

EVERYONE'S GOT A MILLION-DOLLAR IDEA . . . OR SO THEY SAY

Most people never get started.

The reason people don't succeed is not because they don't have great ideas, it's because they never get started. They never take action. They never take the first step.

Do you know how many times I've heard people say, "I have a million-dollar idea" and then do nothing? A lot! Then a couple years go by, and they see a company absolutely thriving, and they say, "That was my idea. I should've been a millionaire."

Well, guess what? Your idea might not have been lacking, but your ability to take action was.

Why does this happen? Why do we have these amazing ideas but never take the plunge? Why do we have these great ideas but give up before we really get started?

Here are some of the biggest reasons:

- fear of failure

- fear of being rejected

- fear of actually succeeding

- fear of being judged

- fear of being uncomfortable

- fear of not being able to provide for their family or pay the bills.

So many of us have this greatness inside of us and know we are capable of so much, yet we tend to hold back. Maybe you're trying to launch your first idea into the world, or maybe you want to go from five figures to six figures or six figures to seven figures. Every stage of entrepreneurship comes with a decision.

Am I willing to commit even though it will be hard, not guaranteed, and require incredible vulnerability?

For some of us, we stop here with our fears. But that's not what an Elevated Entrepreneur does.

An Elevated Entrepreneur is willing to do what it takes even if it challenges them beyond imagination or scares the absolute shit out of them. They are willing to try, even if success isn't guaranteed, because they know their purpose is greater than the regret of not trying at all.

When I was scared to release my first book, *Elevate Beyond*, my dad told me to go for it. He told me that as soon as I put the book into the world, great things would happen. He didn't know what types of things, but he knew that if I took action and did something greater than just myself, the world would produce results for me. Since that day, my life has been full of adventure, excitement, success, and so much more.

I asked many of the guests what they would recommend to someone who has a dream but is holding back from taking the next step. Here are some of the top answers:

Start small and start on things that actually matter.

Stop reading and consuming and start implementing.

Identify the consequence of not starting.

Find one simple thing you can do today, and keep doing it every day after that.

No one is you, and that is your power. Use it to unlock your greatness.

You do not need a permission slip to get started. If you feel that way, get one today from a mentor, coach, or friend.

You're going to die.

Resistance to change is normal because of the unknown. Become aware of this and change loses its power.

Be willing to be uncomfortable and minimize your risk.

Embrace the fear and welcome it. It means you're headed in the right direction.

Tap into your internal compass. Follow the direction it's guiding you towards.

Start with where you are and what you have. Leave the comparison behind because everyone starts at zero and goes up from there.

Burn the ships and figure it out. Go all in!

Think about who you are robbing by not sharing your gifts. You're actually stealing from people, and no one likes to steal.

There is no single road to achieving personal success, but there is one thing you cannot argue with. Every person who ever became successful took action. They took messy action and figured it out along the way.

No one begins with perfect execution, but winners always start. To be an Elevated Entrepreneur, you need to start, and so I challenge you right now to set this book down, write one action you can take that will move the needle in your business and life, and execute on that action.

Kobe Bryant wasn't one of the best basketball players of all time on day one.

Lewis Howes wasn't an industry leader on day one.

Queen B wasn't the world's greatest on day one.

A successful journey takes time, but it always requires you to start.

One of my clients, Kat Norton, a.k.a. Miss Excel, has an incredible story of taking the plunge and getting started. When we first started working together, she was working a full-time job, but on the side, she was making TikTok videos of her dancing and teaching Microsoft Excel tricks. The minute I saw her videos, I knew she had the secret sauce. She wanted to find a way to turn her dancing TikToks into an online business, so during our first month together, I helped her take messy action and create her first program: The Excelerator Course. Since then, her course has become a huge hit and has been purchased all over the world. She has been featured in *Business Insider*, won a Microsoft MVP Award, and had her first six-figure month all within a fairly short period of time.

When you take action, great things happen. Kat didn't know exactly how it would all work out, but she knew to get to the next level, she had to start, and she had to start today. I'm so proud of Kat and the amazing impact she is having on the world. Make sure to check her out at miss-excel.com and on Instagram @miss.excel.

MAHDI WOODARD

Bio

Mahdi Woodard is the founder of the 100K Campaign, a digital learning community created to help entrepreneurs attain and maintain six-figure success across a range of industries. Prior to his entrepreneurial endeavors, Mahdi served in several marketing leadership roles for brands ranging from $250M to $1.2B in revenue. During his corporate stint, he successfully launched over 1,000 SKUs in thirteen different countries. Mahdi holds a Bachelor of Science in Business Administration from Bucknell University in Lewisburg, PA. He is a proud native of Atlanta and currently lives just outside of downtown.

How to Connect

Personal IG: @mahdiwoodard

Business IG: @100kcampaign

Website: 100kcampaign.com

How We Met

Mahdi is a content machine, and I love what he produces. I was intrigued by his approach, so I went straight to the source. I sent him a DM and invited him to be part of this book because I thought he would have a lot to add to my readers. After a few follow-ups and some persistence, he agreed to be featured.

What is the one thing that, if you knew when starting, would have accelerated your path to success?

I had a misconception that because work had to be done, it had to be done by me. One of the things when I first started was that I tried to do everything. I was doing the business development and the operations, and it sort of slowed the progress by not understanding how to break some of the work up.

What are three pieces of software/technology you recommend people use in their business?

ConvertKit

SuperPhone (SMS text messaging marketing)

Iconosquare

Instagram

For somebody who has dreams of being a wildly successful entrepreneur with freedom, what is the most important thing to focus on?

You have to develop some sort of understanding of how long it takes for things to really materialize. That's not to say that other people don't see success sooner or that you can't be one of those people where your first thing automatically works, but oftentimes, some humility in the process—studying other people and seeing what their journey was like— can help you calibrate and set the appropriate expectations for what you're truly signing up for. Once you're clear this thing is not just a hustle, it's not just something that you're trying out, that this is a lifestyle, it's off to the races from there. I would say dream big, work even harder, stay laser-focused, and lastly, always be open to feedback. There are a lot of smart people out in this world, and they can accelerate your growth if you're willing to listen.

No entrepreneurial journey goes from A to B in a straight line. How did you overcome the internal doubts and external adversity along the journey?

There's a quote that says, "If you can make it out of your mind, you can make it anywhere," and oftentimes that is the largest hurdle for us because we're growing up in a society that grooms us. I'm not knocking society, but for it to function, it grooms us to look at these things as what are jobs, what are careers, what are the safest ways to go through this thing called life. You have to reorient and unlearn a lot of the things that you thought to be true. And so internally, it's managing those emotions and not blaming yourself now that you have different information. It's being willing to adjust and make some changes. Externally, I think a lot of things depend on your business model, but what I would say is, "How do I build stronger relationships with real people?" This is ultimately how you stay in the fight and how you can get to the next phase.

What is your definition of success?

Internally, it's the ability to take my imagination, my creativity, and make it real. That's my internal charge every day. How can I continue to imagine things and work on them and make them true?

The external part is, can I help someone else do the same? Oftentimes, you have to make some cash, print a T-shirt, see something in the world you've created for it to feel real. I know that when it starts to feel real and you get that feeling, you are going to be addicted to it.

Most people never get started. What would you say to someone who has a dream but is holding back from making the plunge?

I think everyone has some type of internal compass, and when it won't shut up, when it keeps calling out, I think you owe it to yourself to really give this thing a go. For some people that may look like part-time. For other people, it's going to look like jumping. We've heard the analogy of building it as you fly or building on the way down. You have to get quiet enough in order to hear that voice clearly, but at some point, you're going to have to jump. You're going to have to say this thing is plan A and plan B and plan C. There may be a pivot or change of direction, but my life is this type of work.

How do you relentlessly pursue excellence, greatness, and success (however you define it), while at the same time enjoy the journey of life?

I'm glad you're asking me at this point in my life, because I wouldn't have a genuine answer for you five years ago. I wasn't enjoying it at all. It was a lot of anxiety. It was a lot of not knowing if this thing is going to pan out. Now I have a sense of surety that everything is going to be okay, even if okay isn't the artificial goals that I've set for myself. I stay focused on it by actually writing it out. Give yourself some objectives, some things that can be black and white that someone else can look at and measure you against, but then never forget just how rare this thing is. I'm in the comments, I go live, and I talk to supporters. Take it all in because people need to see this thing, that it's real, that you can be a regular person. I don't come from money. I didn't have any type of fancy connections. You just get here and do your best. For me, it's staying connected with the people that help me manifest my dreams, so whether they're clients, customers, or supporters, I have to touch the people and talk to them and show my appreciation for them.

What is one action you recommend someone do every day to be the best version of themselves?

I would recommend that you actually write out the thing that you're grateful for, whatever that is, on that given day. Some days it's big, and you're grateful to be alive. Other days, you're grateful to have some peace of mind. When you actually write it out and look at it over a period of time, you can see the range of emotions that you've been through. You can see the scale and scope of what life really feels like.

How have relationships—personal and professional—contributed to your success and happiness?

Relationships are everything. I've been called on stages, and I've been pulled into rooms that I had not earned the right to be in yet because of relationships. Someone seeing that you have the potential and extending an opportunity to you, that's been purely because of relationships, and I'm forever indebted. I have a whole list of people I hope to pay back in some way. Professionally, relationships are one of the highest things.

Personally, as an entrepreneur, sometimes you have to bounce things off somebody. You have to talk to a friend. Maybe it's someone that's not even in our world, but asking them "Does this thing sound crazy or does it seem magical?" Having close friends who can sort of cocoon you and wrap around you in a bunch of different ways. I've got friends that pull me out of this thing and ask to go get some lunch and not talk about business. They ask how I'm really doing. Those types of personal relationships keep me in balance.

Who are three of your favorite entrepreneurs to follow, learn from, and/or connect with?

Mia Ray

Myleik Teele

Gary Vaynerchuk

SERENA POON

Bio

Serena Poon, CN, CHC, CHN is a nutritional energy practitioner in which she fuses her expertise as a celebrity chef, nutritionist, and Reiki master to serve her A-list clientele. Serena Loves was launched in 2019, a lifestyle brand, blog, and TV show that encompasses all the pillars of optimal health and well-being. This is achieved through her method of Culinary Alchemy®, which is a combination of education, integrative and functional nutrition, and healing energy. She is also the founder of Just Add Water®, a wellness line of super-nutrient foods and supplements.

How to Connect
IG: @chefserenapoon & @justaddwaterinc
TW: @chefserenapoon & @justaddwaterinc
Website: serenaloves.com

How We Met

I first met celebrity chef and holistic nutritionist Serena Poon after being introduced to her through a mutual friend. I instantly gravitated towards her methods and philosophy in the nutrition, health, and wellness space. I love everything she and the Serena Loves brand stands for and knew I wanted to include her in this book.

What is the one thing that, if you knew when starting, would have accelerated your path to success?

My business has evolved a lot over the years and throughout my journey, and I think that one thing I wished I would've known was that it's okay to make mistakes. That's where you learn, and that's really where the greatness comes.

What are three pieces of software/technology you recommend people use in their business?

Slack

Airtable

Instagram

For somebody who has dreams of being a wildly successful entrepreneur with freedom, what is the most important thing to focus on?

I would say two things. The first is balance. All entrepreneurs know it is one of the hardest things you truly maintain, but that's what's going to lead you to success. Constantly keeping yourself in check and making sure that you're balanced—your work life, your personal life, your self-care, and your health—on every level. The health of your business is going to be a direct reflection of the health of your body. The second would be to set attainable and achievable goals within the realm of possibility. You have to set goals that are within that realm because you want to check off those milestones because it really keeps you moving forward.

No entrepreneurial journey goes from A to B in a straight line. How did you overcome the internal doubts and external adversity along the journey?

My journey started with struggle and challenges, and the reason I started my career is because both my parents had cancer, and then that led into my own personal health issues. I believe it's about surrendering, so really embracing what's right in front of you especially when we have challenges, both internal and external. Internal for me was not just my mind, but it was also my body because I had to deal with some health challenges. External challenges could be a million things from canceling an Instagram LIVE because there were tech issues with Wi-Fi or what happened in 2020 with the pandemic. When you can find a moment to just be super present and see that what's in front of you is this massive challenge and hurdle that you have to get over, you will see all the beauty and the opportunities that are also just right past what's in front of you, and that typically comes from surrender and embracing what is.

What is your definition of success?

Peace and impact. Making an impact means you're bringing value and adding value to people, and you're changing people's lives in the most positive and beautiful way possible. You can have all the money in the world and can drive all the impact, but you need to have peace within yourself because that also goes into the energy of what you do.

Most people never get started. What would you say to someone who has a dream but is holding back from making the plunge?

No one is you, and that is your power. People who have these dreams but don't turn them to reality often think that that power is external. They think that it comes from people or how much money you have, but that power really comes from within you. You're going to be the one that makes your dream your reality. Who is going to put that special secret sauce at the end with your business or your idea is YOU. Someone could take your same idea and it might not turn out exactly the same because it's yours. It's your magic and it's your energy, and that might sound a little woo woo to some people, but that is very much ingrained in everything that I do. It's realizing that you are the force that's going to drive the vehicle the whole way from start to finish.

How do you relentlessly pursue excellence, greatness, and success (however you define it), while at the same time enjoy the journey of life?

Every Sunday, I check in on myself. This is so important especially as an entrepreneur who works so hard. I love what I do, so it's work, but it doesn't feel like work. It's literally putting these self-care blocks on the calendar. Whether it's meditation, exercise, a walk, dinner with a friend, some sort of body work, or whatever it is, it's just checking in and making sure you have your self-care because that brings you balance and keeps you in alignment.

What is one action you recommend someone do every day to be the best version of themselves?

Your morning routine. Every single person I talk to, I tell them to check their hydration. It sounds so crazy simple, but the two things are hydration and meditation/grounding. People don't realize how important it is to stay really well hydrated and do it first thing in the morning and set this as your practice. Most peak performers burn a lot of energy, and they could be on coffee and other caffeinated drinks to help sustain their energy, but half the time, your body just needs water. It sounds so silly, but it's so important, and it has to be part of your morning routine because your routine is what sets you up for success. Sometimes I fall off too, we're all human, but you have to get yourself right back on it because your routine is what gets you to your goal.

How have relationships—personal and professional—contributed to your success and happiness?

I think community and relationships are everything. They're the backbone to who you are as a person, to your development, to the success of not just your personal success but also your business. Learning through my journey, I would have leaned on my relationships more. There are a lot of lessons I've had from personal relationships because they teach you about yourself. These relationships—especially any of the difficult ones you may have had—are all mirrors to what it is that you need to work on. And that's a hard truth to swallow because if you've had a tough relationship with somebody, you want to think it's not you, it's them, but really, they're holding up a mirror to things that you need to heal within yourself. And if you heal those things, it's going to level you up.

From a business standpoint, one thing that I teach my team, mentees, anyone is how you relate to and treat people is everything. We do not live in a world where there's six degrees of separation, and at the end of the day, we are all the same. People ask me about my celebrity clients all the time and how I built my relationship with them, and that's because I've always treated everyone the same. We are all the same, and when you remember that, there's no judgment about anything. So, I have the relationships that I have because I've literally always treated everyone the same—with kindness and compassion. By doing that, it really builds your network in a way that's really beautiful because when you're putting that energy out, you're also bringing that energy in.

Who are three of your favorite entrepreneurs to follow, learn from, and/or connect with?

Tony Robbins

Oprah Winfrey

Jamie Kern Lima

CLAY HEBERT

Bio

Clay Hebert is a marketing and branding strategist, entrepreneur, speaker, and storyteller. As the founder of Take Back Perfect, he loves words, and he believes we make marketing harder than it needs to be. *Forbes* called him "one of the next generations of business and media influencers," and he was recently named one of *Entrepreneur Magazine's* 50 Most Daring Entrepreneurs . . . along with Jeff Bezos and Elon Musk.

Today, through his Perfect Intro, Perfect Brand, and Perfect Stack frameworks, Clay helps leaders, executives, and entrepreneurs tell better stories, grow their companies, fund their dreams, and do work that matters.

How to Connect

IG: @clayhebert

LI: /clayhebert

TW: @clayhebert

Website: clayhebert.com & takebackperfect.com

How We Met

Through Kayleigh Christina.

What is the one thing that, if you knew when starting, would have accelerated your path to success?

There's no one key to success, but if I was starting over, I wish I understood what I call the Five Phases of Entrepreneurship, which is simply about how many customers you have.

Phase One is from zero to one: When you have a brand-new idea—a

93

brand-new business—you're in this phase. All new businesses start with zero paying customers. From zero to one is an entire phase, and it's where many startups die. To get past Phase One, you have to get *one person* that's a stranger (not your mom or your significant other) to pay for your product or service. *Phase Two* is from one customer to ten. That's an entire phase, and it's totally different. You do different things; you make different decisions. *Phase Three* is going from ten people to one hundred paying for your product or service. *Phase Four* is one hundred to one thousand. And *Phase Five* is when you have over one thousand paying customers.

When we start new ventures, we can imagine thousands of customers. We imagine what it's like to launch the next Airbnb and go really, really big. We imagine going from zero to huge, but it never happens that way.

Most new businesses die in Phase 1 or 2 before they have ten paying customers.

Each phase brings new challenges and activities, so whether it's products, services, consulting apps, or a corner bakery, whatever your business is, it's helpful to chunk it down and map out what it takes to get to the next phase.

What are three pieces of software/technology you recommend people use in their business?

I actually built my latest startup to answer this exact question. At PerfectStack.co, there's a tool to help you choose your Perfect Stack of tools for your business. And it's completely, 100% free.

Every business is different, but personally, I couldn't run my business without Slack, Zoom, and ConvertKit (my email service provider).

Also, I know social media is often treated as a distraction and an enormous waste of time, and it can be, but I actually consider Twitter an essential business tool. I've made incredible, life-changing connections via Twitter.

For somebody who has dreams of being a wildly successful entrepreneur with freedom, what is the most important thing to focus on?

This is one of the most important questions, maybe *the* most important.

First, you have to define success. Then, you have to define freedom, because both of those words mean wildly different things to different people.

I call this building your Perfect Calendar.

When we imagine a new venture, it's common to focus on customers, revenue, profit, and growth. But we don't think about the impact on our calendar.

But every new business comes with a different calendar. Figure out what freedom means to you. What do you want to do every week? What kind of meetings do you want to have? With whom? What is the hard part? Which parts light you up? Then make sure the business you want to build can give you the Perfect Calendar you want to live.

The happiest, most successful people in the world wake up every day, look at their calendar, and get excited. I came from a decade of management consulting where I woke up every day double and triple booked with meetings I didn't want. Now I look at my calendar, and I love the meetings I have and the things I get to do.

That's intentional, it makes me happy, and to me, that's both success and freedom.

No entrepreneurial journey goes from A to B in a straight line. How did you overcome the internal doubts and external adversity along the journey?

We all struggle with internal doubts. There's a great riff on imposter syndrome where two guys were sitting in the back being wallflowers at a fancy party.

They're sitting back against the wall, and one guy says to the other, "Look at all these amazing people." The other guy says, "You're pretty amazing yourself." The first guy says, "No, *these* guys are smart. I just went where I was told."

The two guys were Neil Gaiman, one of the best authors of all time, and Neil Armstrong, the first man on the moon.

So, if the first man to step foot on the moon and one of the greatest authors of our generation have imposter syndrome, it's natural that we do as well. I don't think we should try to squash imposter syndrome or eliminate it. I think we should recognize it and welcome it. Let it in, pour it a cup of coffee. Then after five minutes, tell it to get the hell out because you got some work to do.

Speaking is another good example. I do a lot of public speaking, and there can be crippling internal doubts before you walk out on stage. You're imagining that everyone wants you to be entertaining and smart and funny. There's only one thing that can reduce those doubts. It's literally one word: reps.

Just like sports or writing or making YouTube videos, you have to put in the reps. Right now, if you told me that I have to go across the street and give The Perfect Intro keynote to two thousand real estate agents or loan officers, it's no problem. I have the slides. I've done the talk hundreds of times. At this point, it's muscle memory.

It's like a comedian who's been working on one hour of their work every night for a year, and now they're ready to do it on a big stage. I can do it and I have no doubts, but only because of the reps, only because I screwed up and failed, only because smart, generous people gave me good feedback and questions that made it better.

You have to start and do it over and over. You have to do it ugly. Tucker Max calls it the vomit draft of your book because when you're vomiting, you don't care what you look like, you just have to get it out. Great writing is more editing than it is writing, so just vomit the first ugly thing on the page and then start fixing it.

What is your definition of success?

Someone who loves their calendar and the people they spend time with.

Most people never get started. What would you say to someone who has a dream but is holding back from making the plunge?

Figure out the smallest thing that you can do to move that forward. Where we get stuck is when we think about going from zero to Madison

Square Garden. Instead, think about going from zero to hosting a dinner party. What's the smallest thing you can do?

I'll use another analogy. People say, "Well, how do you teach leadership?" That's a big question. How do you teach an eighth-grader leadership? You have them be the one that organizes a movie night for their twelve friends to go to the mall to see the hot, new movie. That's leadership. If you're the kid that is always organizing your friends to go to movies in high school, you're going to be the person who organizes groups or trips in college. These people become leaders in business.

So, what's the smallest thing that you can do to move it forward?

How do you relentlessly pursue excellence, greatness, and success (however you define it), while at the same time enjoy the journey of life?

I think it's the same thing. People say, well how do you pursue success, but they usually equate success to massive wealth. A lot of people think they want Gary Vaynerchuk's success, but they don't want his calendar. A lot of people want Elon's impact and his wealth and his billions, but they don't want his calendar.

It depends on what you call success. There are infinite kinds of success, and I think it's worth sitting down and writing down and saying what success looks like for you while trying to forget everything that Instagram and Twitter and culture and media and *Entrepreneur Magazine* have told us what success is supposed to be. There should be a magazine like *Entrepreneur* or *Fast Company* or *Forbes* where it's just really happy people on the cover who've designed the perfect life for them, and not the latest internet billionaire.

If you want that, and you know the calendar it requires, then go build that. There's no one clever little secret to go build a billion-dollar company, but there's a lot of people who are unhappy paddling towards that billion-dollar company when that's not the life they want anyway because they thought about it in terms of money in the bank and not in terms of how they spend their time.

What is one action you recommend someone do every day to be the best version of themselves?

Work out. Do something. Move your body. It doesn't have to be deadlifts or whatever you're into, but move your body.

Take phoneless walks. Wake up and go for a walk before you get on your phone or laptop. That's one of the best things you can do. The only rule is, no phone. If you want to do it alone, do it alone. If you want to do it with your partner or walk your dog, great, but wake up and before you go down the social media rabbit hole, get outside and just go for a walk.

That's where your next big idea, your startup, your book, that's when clarity of thought is the highest. Jim Kwik says, "when your body moves, your brain grooves," and that's completely true. It's especially true early in the morning and especially true if you're not on your device yet. Leave your phone at home. If you want, bring a little notepad and a pen, and write down the ideas and what comes up.

How have relationships—personal and professional—contributed to your success and happiness?

Relationships are everything. That's number one, because if you think about it, *everyone is someone you met*. That's why I created The Perfect Intro. I'm fascinated with improving conversations and relationships and how we show up and how we tell the story of the work we do and how we impact people. There are infinite resources and books and things like that to get better at interacting with other humans, and it blows me away that people don't take the time to get better at relationships and communication.

Crucial Conversations is an incredible book about how to have the most important conversations in your life. Nobody has crucial conversations every single day, but sometimes we do, whether that's firing a co-founder or breaking up with somebody or getting that job. Get better at relationships because relationships are literally everything.

Who are three of your favorite entrepreneurs to follow, learn from, and/or connect with?

Seth Godin

Tucker Max

JeVon McCormick

Naval Ravikant

Aubrey Marcus

CHRIS DUCKER

Bio

Chris is a serial entrepreneur and author of the best-selling books, *Virtual Freedom,* and *Rise of the Youpreneur.* Based in Cambridge, England, he owns and operates several businesses, including the personal brand education company, Youpreneur.com, which housed over 350 full-time employees. Nowadays, he spends most of his time coaching and mentoring successful entrepreneurs, as well as investing in and advising startup companies.

How to Connect

IG: @chrisducker

FB: /chrisducker

YT: /chrisducker

TW: @chrisducker

Website: chrisducker.com

How We Met

Chris is one of those people who I'd heard of but never really knew too much about. I mean, he lives across the pond in the UK, but as I was researching for this book, his name kept popping up, so I shot him a DM on Instagram to see if he was open to connecting. After a few messages, I realized he was the man! This wasn't just because he's super successful and knowledgeable, but also because he's a big basketball fan, and we were able to connect through our shared interest. I invited him to be in the book, and a few months later, it was scheduled, and we did it!

What is the one thing that, if you knew when starting, would have accelerated your path to success?

Team building without a doubt. That's a very, very easy question to answer. The reason is, I burned out at the end of 2009. At that point, by the way, I had over one hundred staff, we had just hit our first seven-figure revenue year after about three years in business, so I was super pumped, but I was a wreck physically, emotionally, mentally. I was absolutely and completely exhausted, and so when I went through that burnout—we're talking like hospital time, antidepressants, fluids, the whole thing—it became really obvious to me that if I wanted to avoid that going forward and continue to build the business, that there's no way I was going to be able to do it all on my own. I was wearing too many hats, and so at the beginning of 2010, I had a goal to ultimately fire myself from the business. It took eight people to do that, so I hired eight people in eight different roles in 2010 to replace myself in the business, which just shows you how many hats I was wearing. So, without a doubt, the number one biggest, most important thing for anybody who wants to build a powerful, profitable business that's going to be around longer than five minutes, you've got to build your team.

What are three pieces of software/technology you recommend people use in their business?

Basecamp and Asana (project management systems)

Facebook Messenger, WhatsApp, Slack (communication apps)

Dropbox

No entrepreneurial journey goes from A to B in a straight line. How did you overcome the internal doubts and external adversity along the journey?

I think the first thing is that you have to understand that in order to be able to continue to grow, you need to continue to learn, and I think that a lot of people get to a certain level of "success." Now, that word is very subjective because it means something totally different to you than it does to me or anybody else, and so I think you've got to continue to learn, particularly if you want to be a leader of people—a leader in an industry, a leader of other business owners, or whatever it is—in order to continue to lead. That's number one.

Number two is the importance of understanding the power of getting out of your own damn way and putting your hand up and saying, "I need help right now. I can't do this myself."

That's huge, absolutely huge. When you take into consideration that almost all entrepreneurs out there, particularly starting and growing businesses in today's very digital, very online, very connected world, are type A, multiple-hat-wearing, micro-managing disasters ready and waiting to happen. So, when you have the mental capacity to turn around and say, "I can't do this, I need help, I'm going to struggle," that's massive. You can't put a dollar amount on that kind of mindset shift, and so those are the two things right there. I think getting out of your own way and the importance of continuing to learn.

What is your definition of success?

Here's the thing. It's different for everybody. For me, the definition of success as a father of four is to make sure that I can do work that I genuinely enjoy doing every single day, that I work with people that I genuinely enjoy working with, but also that I can step away whenever I want to, like when one of my kids wants to build a LEGO set or do some drawing or go for a walk or feed horses or whatever we do here in the English countryside.

I think that honestly, I'm living it right now, and I have been for several years, but I understand that was not an overnight success. My overnight success took fifteen-odd years to get to. Success is different for everyone. For me, it's about just living life the way you want to more than anything else.

Most people never get started. What would you say to someone who has a dream but is holding back from making the plunge?

Go get a permission slip from someone because generally that is all that they need. I've coached thousands of people through my work, books, courses, and programs to know that nine times out of ten, the reason why somebody doesn't hit the start button on a project or on a goal, regardless of how big or small it might be, is because they haven't had the permission given to them from somebody. Sometimes, it needs to be their spouse or their partner, and sometimes, it needs to be one of their mastermind accountability buddies. Sometimes, it might even be a customer or a client, so the permission is huge. You need to know that perhaps that's what's holding you back a little bit, so go find your permission slip.

How do you relentlessly pursue excellence, greatness, and success (however you define it), while at the same time enjoy the journey of life?

For me, it's about the work that I do through the people that I work with. We have a number of different businesses, so it's not just one business model. We have a large call center facility, a VA recruitment company, and then we have Youpreneur, which is more of the educational business. So, whether it's me working with our executive management on our recruiting and call center side of the business, I will live vicariously through their success. I want to see someone that came in ten years ago as one of my customer service reps step it up and grow a career with me. That's my success. If I can help that person build a career for themselves and their family, I'm happy right there. Likewise, through the educational side of the business and the clients that we coach, we have one particular client based here in the UK. He's been in the digital game for twenty years running his own business, and when he joined the program at the beginning of 2020, I said to him, "Do everything I tell you to do within reason, and I promise you'll have the best year in your twenty years of business. Just do what I tell you to do, and you'll be just fine." And he did, and in September this year, he sent me an email saying this was going to be his best year yet. So, that's the way I like to live through those kinds of wins.

What is one action you recommend someone do every day to be the best version of themselves?

This is a little one but my Mammy who's from Dublin taught me when I was ten years old that I cannot start the day without making my bed. To this day, my wife won't even touch the bed. For me, it's a switching point. It's me turning a switch in my mind that says the bed is made, it's time to get to work.

How have relationships—personal and professional—contributed to your success and happiness?

They're everything. I think personal relationships are more important than business relationships to me, even those personal relationships that have come out of business situations. I'm very, very blessed to be very close friends with very big successful business owners, particularly in the online space, and I would chuck any joint venture, any opportunity, whatever it is, in the bin to keep those personal relationships forever. They're way more important to me. I think people don't put a big enough premium on the importance of relationships, and I believe wholeheartedly that relationships should be treasured, they shouldn't be used. In this kind of startup hustle-and-grind mentality of a world that we live in, too many relationships are being used, and that's not the right way to build a successful mindset in life or business. I think if you genuinely go into relationships for the right reasons with that in mind, then you can't lose.

Who are three of your favorite entrepreneurs to follow, learn from, and/or connect with?

Richard Branson

Gary Vaynerchuk

Zig Ziglar

Bruce Lee

ALLYSON BYRD

Bio

Allyson Byrd is also known as the Profit Accelerator™, and she is celebrated as one of the world's most trusted leadership advisors and sales experts for entrepreneurs and small business owners.

Today, her and her team executive produce exclusive virtual membership communities for influencers with online audiences over one million in reach. Allyson's clients generate a collective thirty-three million dollars in sales revenue annually. She and her team have coached 10,000 entrepreneurial leaders to create $349 million in new revenue over the past thirteen years.

You'll be able to hear more of Allyson's journey to success from an underprivileged life on food stamps, a dad in prison, and single mom raising two kids to the ultra-passionate successful leader she is today and the undeniable stand she has for women rising into their greatness in her latest collaboration with Amazon Prime TV.

Allyson's press features include *CNN, USA Today, NPR, Time Money, Forbes, Yahoo Finance, Business Insider, CNBC, MSN, Black Enterprise, Essence,* and *Entrepreneur.com.*

How to Connect
IG: @iamallysonbyrd

How We Met

Allyson was referred to me by another entrepreneur I respect. I checked out her social media and knew Allyson would be incredible to feature. After a few messages, some persistence, and a quick chat, Allyson agreed to share her wisdom as a featured guest in the book.

What is the one thing that, if you knew when starting, would have accelerated your path to success?

If I were to play it all over, I would have put money at a higher importance. I feel like so much counsel came to me on pursuing mission over money, but when you're first starting a business, you need to be able to pay your rent. You need to be able to pay your mortgage. You need to be able to pay your light bill, and you can't be the light when you're worried about the light bill.

I wish that I would have had somebody in my life tell me that money is important, and to do the thing where you can make money quicker, sooner, and faster. Then, buy your time back and step deeper into your meaning after that. I was trying to be so meaningful at the beginning, but that meaning isn't always monetizable. The thing that you're the most passionate about, the most excited about, that brings you the greatest sense of aliveness isn't always a successful business model, and it's not always something that people are willing to pay for.

I wish that I would have looked at "What are my skill sets that are successfully monetizable? How do I make more money quicker, sooner, and faster? How do I take that money and buy my time back and be more strategic with who I am in the world and give myself permission to achieve in three areas (life provision, professional achievement, and personal fulfillment) and not lump it all into one category called entrepreneurship?" I would have had a lot less personal failure. I would have fatigued my faith a lot less. I wouldn't have been as angry or judgmental, or as driven by comparison as I was. That would have made a big difference for the human that I was for so many years at the beginning of leading my business.

For somebody who has dreams of being a wildly successful entrepreneur with freedom, what is the most important thing to focus on?

I know that I'm the Profit Accelerator, I know that I'm the money mindset expert, and there's a reason why my mind always goes to money. I want to say money, but I'm going to put two answers parallel to each other: money and movement. So, what I believe is that when people start out for entrepreneurship, they do not think about where my customer is going to come from. I guarantee you your customers are not going to be on a recurring channel from your church, from your friend group, or from your gym. They're not going to be in any atmosphere immediate to you. You might get a one-off or two-off, but what will really support you is being able to know how to create a movement and how you get people interested in following you, because if you can get one follower, you can get a hundred, and if you can get a hundred active followers, then you've got raving fans. There was a book years ago called Raving Fans that I loved. One of the things that I think most people don't do is look at how you become a person that influences people in a way that people are interested enough to continue to pay attention to, because if they will pay you attention, they will also pay you money, and you have to know that. If they will give you attention, they will give you a check. For a starting entrepreneur, look at your movement.

You might ask, how do I build a movement? The answer is simple in discovery but challenging in execution. You must master how to be the messenger or spokesperson for your brand.

You have no idea if your idea is going to take off, but the best thing that you can do is start talking about it and see if it meets you back around like gossip. See if it comes back around, and that's how you know your movement has started. The movement is the prelude to the money, and the money is what aligns you with the things you desire to manifest, and those manifestations are what keep you in a series of momentum, and that means life feels good, which means you're operating in new freedoms. That's the highest plight of any entrepreneur... personal freedom while making an impact for the world.

No entrepreneurial journey goes from A to B in a straight line. How did you overcome the internal doubts and external adversity along the journey?

Be where I'm celebrated. When I started early in the game, I had a client who said to me that I was perfect for speaking at her manufacturing society. Now, why did she think I was perfect? She thought I was perfect because she liked me. Here I was, in the south, in my thirties, female, African American, and the demographic of this room of over two hundred people was primarily white or Hispanic, male, and older. I was a young, African American female about to tell them what to do. That doesn't work. When I stood at the front of the room and I felt all of that opposition and resistance, I took that as "you're not good enough, you're not smart enough, you don't deserve the stage, you never should have been here, why did you start this business, why did you think you could make that work?" All the doubts covered me like a blanket wrapped in shards of glass. It was devastating and terrible, but fast forward five years later, and I'm standing at Essence Magazine, the number one magazine for Black women in North America.

Here I am in New York City, in the Time Inc. building, in a sold-out, standing room only room just for me, and the entire room is spilling out. They're so excited no one will move. They're sitting on the floor, and I'm having to squeeze my feet between them. The feedback was extraordinary. No one wanted to leave.

What's the difference? Was I a better speaker, facilitator, trainer from one room over the other? I was still Allyson, but one room wanted me, one room did not. You have to go places where you are celebrated versus tolerated because that tolerance will feed your doubts.

The average human brain has over 60,000 thoughts in a day, and the majority of them are programmed towards the negative. We have to watch feeding that wolf all the time. So, how I started overcoming doubts was to get in places that didn't feed the doubt, get in places that brought me a greater sense of aliveness, that celebrated my identity, that wanted me. That will make such a difference. Don't force yourself where you are not wanted because it will teach you that you are not worthy, and that is not the right lesson. That is not true about any of us, so that was a big lesson of an external force of resistance that then started to speak to me internally, and I had to change that.

When I changed the dialogue inside, I sought better environments outside. Now, I go into places where I know not only do I fit, but I add. When I think about going into Essence and what that felt like—fast forward two years—being in an audience of thousands of women, predominantly none of them people of color, but still knowing that I fit because I was now saying, doing, and being all of myself because I had gone through the manufacturing society and Essence. And now I'd come home to myself, and I carried that validation within. I can go in any culture or any environment now, and I feel good, and I feel valuable, but I still would never subject myself back to that old environment to try to prove a point.

What is your definition of success?

I define success in three ways. I think that most of us define success by what our monetary gain is, but money is not the telltale of success. Freedom is. If you have freedom, then you have success. That's my opinion. But what do you want freedom in? I think it is freedom and power to choose, and so I look at three categories: Do I have freedom and power when it comes to my life provision? Do I have freedom and power when it comes to the things that I want to professionally achieve? Do I have freedom and power when I think about the things that I want personal fulfillment on?

When I look at my personal fulfillment categories, I look at now running a successful non-profit and raising our first million dollars towards specific Black causes and disparities in North America. That's an area of fulfillment and success for me. When I look at professional achievement, I have one of the number one personal development ranked episodes on Amazon Prime and features and partnerships with USA Today and NPR.

Those are things in a professional achievement category that I'm really, really proud of. When I look at life provision, I look at co-founding a tech company, running a successful seven-figure brand, and then also all that I'm able to do with all of the clients that we support. Over the last thirteen years, we've taken ten thousand students through our courses, trainings, and curriculum, and they've generated $349,000,000 in new money. That's their money, not my money. Those are things that help me realize I've created a life of success. Those three categories I'm always looking at. Am I fulfilled personally? Am I provided for? Do I have provision for my life and the lifestyle that I desire? Am I anchored professionally with achievements that matter for me? If I can say yes, yes, yes, or if I can identify gaps or breaches, then that tells me the path to go in the way to walk and how to solve for it and be strategic in that.

What is one action you recommend someone do every day to be the best version of themselves?

Master talking to yourself and speaking well of yourself every single day. Master adjectives that describe exactly what you want to experience. When I wake up in the morning, the first thing that I say to myself is, "It's a good day. It's a really good day. It's a really good day for me." When I'm doing my morning routine, I'm saying to myself what I want out of this day. The first thing that I start with is the emotions I want to feel. I'll start talking about hope, peace, joy, congruence, understanding, compassion, or communication.

If I look at my calendar and I know I'm going to be with my partner, I ask, What do you want to express? How do you want to be seen? What feels like respect? What feels like acknowledgment? What could they say or do or be for you that would be of benefit? What could you say or do or be for them that would be a benefit? I think too many times we stifle our thoughts in our heads, and we don't let them come out of our mouths, and our mouth is so powerful. So, every day that I master talking to myself, what I'm really doing is mastering prophesying for telling, speaking into my future, future pacing, and it's very rare that a day shape shifts into something that I did not speak.

I know that that feels like a soft skill. It feels like something you can't grip, but I promise you that if anyone listening gives themselves permission to say, "When was the last time I spoke to myself about myself and about my day and all I did was speak well, all I did was speak of how good I would feel, how much respect I would have, how much honor I would give to others, and how I could show up in the best possible way as the best human possible? When was the last time I did that?" If your answer is never, then don't tell me my shit doesn't work, it does.

How have relationships—personal and professional—contributed to your success and happiness?

Relationships are the highest currency of your life. There is nothing greater, so they're magnanimous.

Who are three of your favorite entrepreneurs to follow, learn from, and/or connect with?

Jay-Z

Elon Musk

Oprah Winfrey

DAILY ACTIONS TO BE THE BEST VERSION OF YOURSELF

If there's one thing you can learn from this book, it's that there is no single way to build your business and become the entrepreneur you've always wanted to be.

Whether you want to be the next Jon Gordon, Lori Harder, or any of the amazing people featured in this book, you choose the path.

Natasha Bedingfield said it best in her hit song "Unwritten": "Today is where your book begins, the rest is still unwritten." Your journey up to this point in life has led you to reading this very word, but as soon as you put this book down, the next action is up to you.

While there is no right way to live life or achieve entrepreneurial success, there are actions that can help you be the best version of yourself every day.

The key is not doing what other people do for the sake of doing them; it's doing what works for you. I always tell my clients and those around me that just because it worked for them doesn't mean it's going to work for you. Test and experiment all the ideas, and once you've done that, commit to what works best for you based on the definition of success you have.

Oftentimes, we tend to think that the actions we take need to be massive, but in reality, the actions need to be consistent. In Atomic Habits by James Clear, he shares a chart showing that if you improve by 1 percent each day, then over the course of a year, that 1 percent daily improvement creates a 37x growth.

Part of being an Elevated Entrepreneur is figuring out what works for you so you can create the life of your dreams, not someone else's.

One of the traps I see entrepreneurs fall into is wanting to help everyone so badly that they don't take care of themselves. While I love that you care and want to change the world, you have to take care of yourself. As Jay Ferruggia mentions, you have to put on your own oxygen mask first. To be the best for others and deliver at optimal performance levels, you have to take care of yourself.

Here are some ideas you can do daily to be the best version of yourself as inspired by our experts:

- Start and end the day with your family.

- Tell someone you love them.

- Make your bed in the morning.

- Remember your priorities. Humans first. Never sales first.

- Put pen to paper in some way.

- Journal.

- Write out the things you're grateful for.

- Take a walk with a good question in your head.

- Meditate.

- Spend time in silence.

- Master talking to yourself.

- Look in the mirror at the end of the day and be honest with yourself.

- Work on your internal self as self-awareness is the first step to any kind of change.

- Create a document that outlines what your higher self is, who they are, and what character is most effective and aligned to carry the responsibility of what you plan to create.

- Get outside.

- Exercise.

- Develop the perfect morning.

- Get a decent amount of sleep each night.

- Feed your body with the right things: food, drink, positive mindset.

- Hydrate.

- Spend an hour doing deep work without distractions.

Remember, the actions you take create results you desire. When you focus on taking actions that propel you forward, success follows.

STEVE SISOLAK

Bio

Steve Sisolak was born into a working-class family in Milwaukee, Wisconsin, where his parents, Ed and Mary, worked hard to provide for their three children. Steve inherited their blue-collar ethic, working full-time to put himself through college at the University of Wisconsin-Milwaukee. Steve then enrolled in UNLV's graduate studies program, where he received a master's degree in 1978.

Steve put down roots in Las Vegas, built his own communications business, all while raising his two daughters on his own as a single father. Both his daughters attended Nevada's public high schools and UNLV, where Ashley earned her law degree and Carley earned her master's degree.

Motivated by his passion for education, Steve decided to give back to the community that supported him by serving on the Nevada Board of Regents for ten years. As a champion for parents and students, Steve stood up for Nevadans wrongfully charging out-of-state tuition and fought for increased state funding. Education remains a top priority for Steve as governor.

In 2008, after ten years as a university regent, Steve was elected to the Clark County Commission, where he served as chairman until being sworn in as governor of Nevada. On the commission, Steve was known as a coalition builder and problem solver. Steve successfully managed the state's largest county budget and led the county through the recession of 2008. As governor, Steve is working to strengthen Nevada's statewide economy by diversifying our industries and working to attract new fields and recruit job-creating companies to the Silver State.

Steve is proud to be able to call Nevada home and is honored to serve our families as their governor. Throughout his time in office. Steve's goal is to keep Nevada strong and moving forward by investing in education, creating jobs by diversifying the economy, and guaranteeing quality, affordable health care for all Nevadans.

113

> **How to Connect**
>
> TW: @govsisolak
>
> Governor's Office Website: gov.nv.gov/contact/contact

How We Met

Over the last decade, I've had the privilege to work NBA Summer League and be a part of their 130-person on-site staff. When I first started working with them, I had no idea who anyone was or who their parents were . . . which I'm so grateful for. The first year I was there, I met Carley and we hit it off. We became good friends, and for a few years, we developed our relationship. Only a few years later did I even know who her dad was. When this book idea popped up, I felt it was appropriate to ask for the intro and see if I could get her dad, a.k.a. the governor of Nevada, in the book. She was happy to make the intro, and after several months of planning, I drove to Las Vegas from LA and interviewed Steve in the Governor's Office in Las Vegas.

What is your definition of success?

I think my definition has changed a bit over time. You're a little bit more material oriented when you are younger, and I think as you get older, you mature a little bit. My father gave me some advice before he passed: try to make the world a little bit better than it was. And that's what I try to base my life on.

How do you relentlessly pursue excellence, greatness, and success (however you define it), while at the same time enjoy the journey of life?

Well, you have to make time for yourself and the journey and enjoy it. I found that time with both my daughters, Carley and Ashley, and of course my wife, Kathy. They're my rocks, and they're the ones I really go to for support and for encouragement. They never ask for anything. They're just givers, so that's where I find my peace and solitude—my family.

What is one action you recommend someone do every day to be the best version of themselves?

One action I do every day is pray. I start my morning with prayer and end it with prayer because I find peace with that. There are some things that are in your control and some things that are out of your control, and I think that's a good way to start. I also try to have a smile on my face for somebody. You can make somebody's day pretty easy. It's as simple as opening the door for someone, letting them cut in line in front of you, or just a wave or a hello. Little things can make a big difference in a person's life.

How have relationships—personal and professional—contributed to your success and happiness?

Tremendously. It's made me grow tremendously through my experiences. You go through a lot in life. You've got people in your life that make a positive impact and you try to stay away from people that make a negative impact. You can surround yourself with good energy, or you can surround yourself with bad, negative energy. And that's what I've done in my job now and in my other jobs. I have the absolute best staff in the whole world in the governor's office. I surround myself with people that are a lot smarter than me and that know their business a lot better than I do, and I work with them and give them the ability to do their jobs. That makes me better, it makes them better, and it makes the service we provide much better too.

BEN NEWMAN

Bio

Ben Newman is a performance coach, international speaker, and best-selling author whose clients include Fortune 500 companies around the world, business executives, sales organizations, and professional athletes in the NFL, PGA, NBA, MLB, UFC, and NCAA.

Through his speaking engagements, coaching, social media, books, and *The Burn* podcast, Ben has empowered individuals and groups all over the world to reach their championship mindset. As a powerhouse storyteller, Ben moves individuals to think bigger on an emotional level to drive habits that lead to growth. No matter the stage or platform, whether it's serving as the mental conditioning coach for the 18-time National Champion Alabama Crimson Tide football team, or coaching the world's top financial advisors, Ben's powerful message focuses on one goal: to help people maximize both personal and professional success.

How to Connect

IG: @continuedfight

FB: /continuedfight

YT: /bennewman

TW: @continuedfight

Website: bennewman.net

How We Met

When I think of people who absolutely dominate the game of life, Ben comes to mind. I had never met him before, but I thought, "What better way to get access to him than to feature him in my book?" I know he is a no-nonsense guy, so I sent him a super straightforward, no BS DM and invited him to be featured. He got back to me shortly, and we scheduled the interview within a few weeks.

What is the one thing that, if you knew when starting, would have accelerated your path to success?

Don't wait, and go for it sooner. Let me frame that answer. I was actually a financial advisor for over ten years, and my ability to start doing what I was doing as a speaker and coach was a result of getting off to a fast start as an advisor. Back in 2006, I was hired to speak for the first time because I got off to this fast start setting records for a Fortune 100 financial firm here in St. Louis, Missouri. The next thing you know, you start speaking, and you fall in love with it, and you start doing more of it. Fast forward to today, and it's what I do full-time. Everything always happens in the right timing, and I feel blessed to have had the career that I had to set the foundation to do what I do now.

What are three pieces of software/technology you recommend people use in their business?

Success Log

iPad

Notes app

For somebody who has dreams of being a wildly successful entrepreneur with freedom, what is the most important thing to focus on?

Show up and do what you say you're going to do every single day. Think about how many times somebody tells you they want to be great and here's what they're going to do. Think about how excited they get. For me, to figure out how bad you really want it, let me have a conversation with your actions. Let me see how you've shown up the last thirty days. Let me see how you've shown up the last six months. Your actions on a daily basis will help me better understand how bad you really want it. There has to be extreme alignment and attacking of the process every day.

No entrepreneurial journey goes from A to B in a straight line. How did you overcome the internal doubts and external adversity along the journey?

We all have fears, doubts, and uncertainties. I think, over time, I've tried the best I can to shorten the conversations that I have with myself. When

I was younger, I'd have these long conversations wondering, "How am I ever going to get out of this?" Over time, you realize the control we have over our minds to reframe and shift our perspective.

My mother passed away from a rare muscle disease called Amyloidosis eleven days before my eighth birthday. When I think back to my mother's connection to her purpose to continue to lead her two boys, regardless of the pain she experienced and after getting divorced from my father when I was six months old, it's powerful. Every night, without fail, once my mother's bedroom was converted into a hospital, twenty-four-hour nursing care in the house, my mother would come to the dinner table with an IV stand every single night, sometimes it took one nurse, sometimes it took two. And she would ask my brother and me how our days were. I've learned to shift the perspective around my fears, doubts, and uncertainties, and if you tell me, we're not going to do this event together or this isn't going to work out or the budget doesn't work or the date doesn't work or some piece of adversity, I'm going to keep moving because I'm connected to this Burn. Externally, we're all going to face challenges and adversity, but we all have challenges and adversity that have caused us to have perspective to help us fight.

What is your definition of success?

Success is your ability to get back up one more time than you've been knocked down. One of the things that I share, whether I'm with Kansas State football, Alabama football, any of our NFL players, or any of our corporate clients is for that person to have the ability to look in the mirror at the end of the day and say, "Today, I gave it my very best." And if you can honestly drive self-accountability and you have given it your best, you can never ask any more of yourself than your very best, and nobody can ask any more of you than your very best. The tough part is showing up and being honest with yourself to give your best every single day because it's easy to be seduced by success. When things are going well, it's easy to say, "I'll pull back from these behaviors, look how great things are going." The reality is, if you want more of that success, you have to continue to be disciplined because discipline wins.

Most people never get started. What would you say to someone who has a dream but is holding back from making the plunge?

The first thing is to take action. Don't hold back. You have to take action. Oftentimes, your big goal, your big dream, your big vision is in alignment with something that you've already achieved, so if it's in alignment with something you've already achieved, then set the vision, set the goal, and then let's reverse engineer what the goal is. Ask yourself, "What can I do every day that I can control? What's the habit? What's the discipline that, in alignment, if repeated consistently, will give me a high probability of achieving my vision?"

How do you relentlessly pursue excellence, greatness, and success (however you define it), while at the same time enjoy the journey of life?

It's by having balance. It's living up to a Prizefighter Day. I have met speakers and coaches that have great tools and great ideas that they share, but they are not living the things that they teach. I found for me, the way a Prizefighter Day was created was because I learned that that's how I was able to show up and win every day. I connect to my Burn every single morning, and I do it in a couple of ways. On your phone, you have an alarm, and on the alarm, you can actually name your alarm. So, my alarm is named, "Janet Fishman-Newman Legacy." The first thing I see when I wake up is my Burn. I then write my Burn down in my journal, so I'm connecting to that Burn every single day. The moment I say "Janet Fishman-Newman Legacy," there's no going back to bed, no hitting the snooze, no, hey, I'm going to waste the day.

I've intentionally designed my calendar for my morning routine which sets the tone for everything. I do everything I need to do before my kids wake up, which enables me to help my kids get breakfast, drive my kids to school, do the things that allow me to be an active father rather than a father that says, "I'm going to go to the gym, see you kids later." Everybody has a choice how they want to live their lives, but for me, I have to make the sacrifice to spend that time with my kids because I'm on the road a lot. If I'm on a sideline or in a boardroom, I'm gone, so I want to be active when I'm home, and then that sets the tone for the day to then be able to do the things I want to do. My days end at five o'clock at the latest, so I can take my kids to soccer and basketball and be home to sit at the dinner table when I'm in town. I'm very intentional with my time in order to make sure that I can do the things that are important to me in all areas in my life. By sharing this, I hope you're seeing an example that you too can have balance.

What is one action you recommend someone do every day to be the best version of themselves?

Look in the mirror at the end of the day and be honest with yourself. This is not some complex thing. I'm not saying you need to do four hundred things in a day. It could be one thing personal, one thing professional, and one thing that's of service. To keep it simple, identify the most important disciplines, and at the end of the day look in the mirror and be honest with yourself. Did you do it or did you not do it? In the event you fall short, just ask yourself why. Don't go to bed telling yourself that you're a loser, and don't go to bed being negative. You don't have to do that.

I learned a great question from one of my coaches and my mentors, Dr. Jason Selk. If you fall short at the end of the day, ask yourself, "What can I improve tomorrow based upon my performance today?" He helped me learn that that type of a question is a positive, so even though you fall short, you acknowledge you didn't do what you said you were going to do, but why. Why did I not do it? You ask this, so tomorrow, you don't repeat it, and I think far too often people don't evaluate their behaviors or don't have that honest assessment, and because of that, they keep falling short. If you take too many days in a row falling short, then you're going to fall massively, massively short of the things that you want to achieve.

How have relationships—personal and professional—contributed to your success and happiness?

It's everything. I can't stress enough the importance of having relationships, of having a circle of people that you trust. My two high school basketball coaches are still mentors, and I write about them in my books. I played for these guys twenty-four years ago, and they are still so important. Relationships to me are everything. It's a blessing for people to trust me and to share their issues with me. I love the people that I work with, and it's gotten to a point where if I don't have a deep relationship, we can't work together because we have to be able to go to a place of trust and depth. I still have two coaches; I read books every day. I'm far from figuring this thing out, so I think relationships are everything.

Who are three of your favorite entrepreneurs to follow, learn from, and/or connect with?

Jon Gordon

Dr. Jason Selk

Ed Mylett

Andy Frisella

RACHEL BELL

Bio

Rachel is a serial entrepreneur and the founder of Online Coach University, a business mentorship platform that teaches hundreds of online coaches how to build six-figure businesses through social media. At just twenty-four years old, Rachel herself has grown two 7-figure businesses—without spending a dime on advertising. She is on a mission to help coaches leverage the power of social media to build profitable online businesses that they love.

How to Connect

IG: @rachelbell

FB Group: 6 Figure Coaching Biz

Website: onlinecoachaccelerator.com

How We Met

When you hear someone's name over and over again, they must be doing something right. I followed Rachel on IG to see her journey, and without knowing her, I sent a cold email to her team inviting her to be featured in the book. We connected and got the interview on the books. This is a perfect case of success rewards speed, as our relationship is just starting but our impact is ever growing.

What is the one thing that, if you knew when starting, would have accelerated your path to success?

When I was first starting, what I needed to understand and what I got continuously beat over the head with was that it wasn't just a business development journey, it was a personal development journey. I was frustrated and asking, "Why am I not getting the results I want? What's happening? Why is this happening to me?" What I failed to realize was that it was a direct mirror into my internal world, and so when I wasn't getting a client on a sales call because I was intimidated and I didn't want to be perceived a certain way, or I was being passive and submissive, I was trying to isolate the actions themselves from how I was actually being. I was trying to isolate the doing from the being, not realizing that they're not only related, but intertwined, and they affect each other so directly. If I had to give myself one piece of advice in the beginning, it would be to look at my business as a vehicle for personal development, and then the answers will become naturally clear.

What are three pieces of software/technology you recommend people use in their business?

Asana

Toggl

Google Drive

Zapier

For somebody who has dreams of being a wildly successful entrepreneur with freedom, what is the most important thing to focus on?

The first question that I would ask someone who's in a rush is, "Why are you in such a rush?" That's something to get really honest about because your ego really wants the validation of saying that you reached a certain point in a certain amount of time, but that's a never-ending hole. Get clear on that first.

Now, if you're focused on speed and you're focused on longevity, those are two different things that can work harmoniously, but not often. My preferred route is always thinking long game first. Where is your business going to be, not just ninety days from now but in five years from now? What does that look like? What have you built? I think the number one thing to focus on in order to make speed of growth and longevity and sustainability of growth possible is focusing on delivery and doubling down on your client results because that in and of itself can be your marketing machine. If you know how to deliver results, and you're the best in your industry at delivering a specific result to a specific type of person, they are going to be so overly willing to refer you to other people in their circles. If you can really focus on customer delivery and delivering not just a five-star experience but going above and beyond and doing everything in your power to deliver a six-star experience and learning what that is to your clients, you'll have a natural organic marketing machine.

One thing to be really clear about is that referrals and word-of-mouth marketing is not only the most effective way to get clients predictably and sustainably, but also the most time-tested strategy that is in existence. One thing that will never change is how satisfied customers are and how they refer that service or that product to other people who could use it because they're so pleased with how it went.

No entrepreneurial journey goes from A to B in a straight line. How did you overcome the internal doubts and external adversity along the journey?

When you have expectations, you're setting yourself up for suffering. What I like to do every single day is to have standards, not expectations. Standards are usually internally focused like, "How am I showing up today," "How am I being the example," "What is my baseline of happiness," "How am I sourcing my happiness and my satisfaction and my significance?" because if it's sourced in how your business is going or how your clients feel or how your audience feels about you, you're at the mercy of so many unpredictable and uncontrollable factors. It's going to be ridiculous for you to expect that happiness can occur for you every single day, and the truth is, we all just want to be happy. That's the only reason why we are doing anything in life. I know it sounds cliché, but it's true. If you think about what $100 million would do for you, or you think about what the perfect friend circle would do for you, or the perfect clients would do for you, it's all to achieve this sense of well-being and happiness.

What we fail to understand is that that's available to us at any point in time as long as we set our expectations at the floor. I woke up today. I'm alive. I'm in a healthy body. I have ears to listen to this information. I have eyes to read this information. I have a brain that can process this information and learn. Those are things to be incredibly grateful for. I have clean water to drink. I have a roof over my head. I have a freaking smart computer in my hand that can do anything and access any information at any point in time I want. These things are amazing, and we lose our connection to how beautiful and amazing and significant life is just as it is. That's something that I can talk about, and it sounds really cool, and it makes me sound really woke, but the reality is I'm not there most days, which is why I have to set intentional time to meditate and get at base level. What am I grateful for today that has nothing to do with external factors? Because as long as I'm reliant on that, I'm not going to be in control of my own emotional state.

I also think that the emotions you experience in life are a spectrum, and if you're going through your one and only human life trying to restrict the spectrum of emotion and experience that you can have, you are not going to reach the end point, whether that's on your deathbed or you're rocking on your chair as an old man or woman, and be satisfied with what you missed out on. The only reason, oftentimes, we don't take risks or that we don't enter in relationships that we really want or that we don't put ourselves out there and express ourselves for who we really are is because we have these fears that it won't work out in our favor. We fear a certain spectrum of the emotional experience we can have as bad. If I feel sadness, rejection, humiliation, that's bad. I don't want to go there, so then we restrict our actions to only go through a certain lane of life, and we all know how that ends up. My strategy is not only just to be in control of my happiness internally, but also to just know and not be surprised that I'm going to feel depressed sometimes. I'm going to feel anxious sometimes. I'm going to feel blissful, happiness, joy, wonder, awe. I'm also going to feel fear. I'm going to feel scared. I'm going to feel embarrassed. I'm going to feel hurt. I'm going to feel alone. I'm not interested in restricting my human experience. I'm interested in becoming as efficient as I can with my bounce back time. How can I go through these waves of unpredictability and still feel calm, centered, grounded, and open, and loving at the same time? That's a task, I think, that if humans really invested time and effort into, we'd have a much better world.

What is your definition of success?

My definition of success is experiencing a version of life, relationships, and purpose that match your personal desires, not the desires of what the external world places upon you.

Most people never get started. What would you say to someone who has a dream but is holding back from making the plunge?

I'm going to take it back to this one and only human life. You may believe in reincarnation. You may come back as a beautiful little flower or a butterfly or a person who's in a much more privileged position or a person who's in a much less privileged position. Who knows what happens after we die? The fact is, everyone dies, and I've become really, really sobered by this idea of mortality in my life because I understand that it's an illusion that life is a long, guaranteed timeline.

I don't know if you've had this experience in your life, but I've had people taken out of my life very quickly and unexpectedly, and it's the biggest wake-up call ever because you realize, wow, that could happen to anyone. It could happen to me, and I don't want anyone to take risks and exert themselves out of the fear of dying, but I want you to take risks and exert yourself from the pure appreciation and celebration that you get to live, and you get to live now. What would it look like if you weren't afraid to do what you want to do right now? What would it look like if you just did what you wanted to do? You free yourself from the conditioning and the expectations that you think you need to play by the rules. Those rules are actually not your rules. If someone is scared to start, that's okay. I think it's totally okay that you're scared. I think it's natural that you're scared. I think it's good that you're scared. It's scary. You know what else? It's worth it, and it's exciting, and the more appetite you have for risk and uncertainty, the more fun you will have in life, period. I think it's a worthwhile endeavor to expand your capacity for the amount of risk and fear that you can dance with so that you can have everything that you want in life and experience the beautiful parts of life that you wouldn't have gotten to experience if you were just scared.

How do you relentlessly pursue excellence, greatness, and success (however you define it), while at the same time enjoy the journey of life?

My definition of success, for me personally, is enjoyment, period. If I'm not enjoying my life right now, why am I doing what I'm doing? I think there's a time for grit and hustle and grind and all this hard-core blood and guts business mindset. I get it, and I love that, and that's why I do it. If I was torturing myself trying to get to a certain point in my life, I'm a hippy at heart, I couldn't really do that for long before it starts to take a serious mental health toll on me. So, even when I'm grinding and I'm putting in seventeen-hour workdays, which I do, it's something that I love. I always ask myself this question: What would I rather be doing? I'm choosing to build this ecosystem and this empire because it's what I would rather be doing, but the moment that that shifts and I would rather be laying outside in the sunshine, I'll just go ahead and do that knowing that it will fuel my energy to put back into my business when I'm ready to work on it.

What is one action you recommend someone do every day to be the best version of themselves?

Create a document that outlines what your higher self is, who they are, and what character is most effective and aligned to carry the responsibility of what you plan to create. You have to ask yourself every single day, "What is the character that is most effective and aligned to carry the responsibility of what I want to create and act in alignment with who that person is?" You will have to reinvent yourself every single day to break the past conditioning of how you've been raised and what money means and who you are and what you can't be and what you can be. You need to restructure that to ascend to the level that you want to experience. What I use is something called an Upward Spiral Guide, where I go through an entire PDF every single morning of who I want to be, what my core values are, my manifesto of what I want to create in my life, the relationships that I want to have, and how I want to show up in all of the scenarios—whether they're testing me or they're rewarding me—and all of the things that I want to experience or that I'll have to experience on this path. Get really clear on who the character is that you need to play in this lifetime and how that supports you and aligns with you each and every day.

How have relationships—personal and professional—contributed to your success and happiness?

I think relationships are a currency. There are a few different currencies in business that you can focus on building. One of them is money. Another one is audience and community. Another one is relationships. People always say, "it's not what you know, it's who you know," and we always shake our heads, but it is true. The reason why that's important to accept and understand, even though it might piss you off sometimes because it's not fair, is that people connect to people first and foremost. If you are going to be a person worth connecting to, you need to focus on what that person is and how you need to become that person. What are the gaps in which you're not acting in alignment with that?

Similar to my business being a mirror of who I am and where I have room to grow, my relationships do the same thing for me. When you invite someone into a relationship with you, whether it's romantic or plutonic, you're giving them a certain access to you and access to your essence and who you truly are, and that can feel vulnerable, especially if you're doing it right, which is showing them your authentic self. They have the opportunity to hurt you. They have the opportunity to betray you. They have the opportunity to do a lot of terrible things for you and to you. They also have a lot of opportunities to teach you what you need to experience so that you can become who you want to become. That's all life is about in my opinion. You'll hear me talk a lot about becoming because there is no destination. At the end the destination is death, and I'm pretty sure none of us want to get there until we have to, so what is it really about? It's about the never-ending process of becoming. Relationships support me in understanding where I am messed up in the head. Where am I doing a really good job? Who am I really, and where can I offer that feedback to other people as well?

Who are three of your favorite entrepreneurs to follow, learn from, and/or connect with?

Tony Robbins

Patrick Lencioni

Suzy Batiz

CHAD COLLINS

Bio

Chad Collins is a Guinness World Record holder for ticket sales and has generated over $30 million in sales for his live event productions and e-commerce businesses.

His live event production company produces nationally acclaimed family events such as Comic Con for Kids and Brick Fest Live, a LEGO fan experience that has attracted over one million total attendees.

Chad, his work, and his live events have been featured in *TIME for Kids*, CNN, Fox and Friends, and *USA Today*. Chad was also featured in Gary Vaynerchuk's New York Times best-selling book, *Crushing It*.

How to Connect

IG: @chadcollins.me

Website: openworldevents.com

How We Met

It was late 2018, and I was prepping for the 2019 Professional Basketball Combine. We were going to throw our first PBC Influencer game, and I wanted to learn more about selling tickets to live events. My good friend, Alexis Teichmiller, knew Chad was an absolute legend when it came to this and made the intro. We immediately hit it off and over the last few years, we've stayed in touch. Chad has helped with some big introductions and has always been willing to share his knowledge. He is an incredible guy, so when I was writing this book, I texted Chad, and we made this happen.

What is the one thing that, if you knew when starting, would have accelerated your path to success?

Hiring the right people early on. It's really hard to know if something is going to really take off or not take off because we all try different things, and you don't know what thing is going to pop. When our live events business began to pop, there were a bunch of people that were in my circle that we just kind of decided, let's go, and a bunch of people jumped on for the ride, which was great. If I were to take a step back though, I would have made sure that one of the first people I brought on was someone that could understand what the vision was in my head, and then be able to go implement that as an operator for me, so I could live in visionary land for a longer period of time.

What are three pieces of software/technology you recommend people use in their business?

Twilio (text messaging marketing)

Autopilot

Canva

For somebody who has dreams of being a wildly successful entrepreneur with freedom, what is the most important thing to focus on?

It's not the money, believe it or not, because a lot of people equate wild success as an entrepreneur to dollars. What I would say and what I focus on is experiences. I want to go to the grave with the experiences that I was able to provide for my family, my company, and everyone that works for my company. Not only that but all of the clients that we have. When I talk about clients, I'm talking about the tens of thousands of attendees that show up to our events. I'm in the experience business, and I live my personal life that way too. So, to me, success is being able to create some meaningful memories not only for yourself but for the people that are the most important to you, and the people that are most important to me are obviously my family and then every single person that we hire and every client that we have.

What is your definition of success?

I love this question because it means something different in every stage of your life and in every stage of your entrepreneurial journey. Success in the beginning can be closing that first deal or getting the first client. Success later on could be training your team so they now can do this thing that allows our leadership team to accomplish much more.

I was out to lunch with one of my employees once, and he said, "Chad, I want you to know that I'm one of your happiest employees. I come to work every day and I'm happy. I love the stuff that I'm working on. I never had opportunities like this before. You give me the ability to make my own decisions. You must be so proud of how successful you are." I said, "If you were to ask all of your friends, how many people do you think are as happy as you right now?" And he couldn't . . . I said, "That's success. Your attitude right now is what success is."

Success is happiness. If you can wake up every day and you're happy and you're passionate about what you're focused on and the people you're having an impact on, that success. It's not about how big is the business? How much money do I have in my bank account? That's bragging rights stuff, and that's not success. Success is how you feel every day because you could be in a terrible financial situation, but as long as you can get up and you put a smile on your face and are genuinely excited and you feel that energy to turn whatever is bothering you around, that to me is success.

How do you relentlessly pursue excellence, greatness, and success (however you define it), while at the same time enjoy the journey of life?

I think that truebred entrepreneurs, by default, have this personality type where they just go, go, go, go, go, and they may leave a little bit of a wake behind them as they go, but that makes them happy, that drives them. I think a truebred entrepreneur really doesn't need to be told how to be happy. They know what success is. They know what success feels like, and that's why they're so driven to go get it. That's why they ask questions and seek help and are happy to pay for people to solve issues that they have. They're not afraid to ask for help. They're not afraid to try something and have it break. To me, that's all part of that feeling of an entrepreneur.

What is one action you recommend someone do every day to be the best version of themselves?

Tell someone you love them.

How have relationships—personal and professional—contributed to your success and happiness?

They're everything. Relationships are everything. Personally, I met my wife when I was thirteen years old. We didn't date until after we were both in college, but I've known her forever. The fact that we have that history and our families have that history together is huge. By the way, my real entrepreneurial journey with this business doesn't start without her saying it's cool. I remember being on my way to my nine to five job, and I got a text message about a project I was working on. I didn't reply to the text, and I called my wife and told her today is the day we've been talking about. She asked if I was sure, and I said the worst case is this other thing doesn't work out, and I just go back to work. She said all right. That is huge from a personal relationship standpoint.

Professional relationships—I'll go back to what we did on YouTube. We go on YouTube, we meet all these people, we build a community, and then after the community is already built, after all the sweat equity is there, we say we're going to have this even—and you have to pay to come to the event—but we're having this event. If you are able to build a community and you're able to consistently deliver and add value and entertainment and make them laugh and make them cry, and the people that are in your world feel a deep connection with you, and then you let them know you're thinking about doing this thing and ask if they'd be interested, they're going to be excited.

You best believe that if you are able to build a connection, other people want to participate in the things that you have going on, and they're going to be there for you. I look back on it, and I understand that that's what happened then, but I'll tell you, that's not what I thought was happening then. We were building our channel out of love and joy and family time. We just so happened to have people also watch it and be engaged, and we just so happened to want to bring everyone together to have an event. Of course, that just spiraled into what it has become, but community building comes first. After you build a community, the sale or the offer or the product or service that you go back to your community to talk about, them buying it is the easy part as long as you did all that leg work to establish yourself within that certain community or create a community on your own.

Who are three of your favorite entrepreneurs to follow, learn from, and/or connect with?

Eben Pagan

Russell Brunson

Jeff Walker

Tim Ferriss

KENZIE BURKE

Bio

In a few short years, Kenzie Burke has become an inspirational force for people seeking to take their wellness and well-being into their own hands. While best known for her 21-Day Reset program and her dedication to awaken and share what she learns along the way, Kenzie's brand has evolved to include an organic and biodynamic superfood product line, a highly successful podcast, and her biggest and most ambitious project yet: the creation of the FOR YOU app.

FOR YOU by Kenzie Burke is an inspiring guide to unearthing and aligning with the body and life that one may truly desire. By exploring the infinite power of foods and providing you with an abundance of simple, plant-based recipes, extraordinary tools, and transformative methods and programs designed to reshape your everyday. FOR YOU is the bridge to an abundant, alluring, rich, and powerful life.

Kenzie invites you to follow her journeys and creations at:
kenzieburke.life

How to Connect
IG: @kenzieburke
Website: kenzieburke.life

How We Met

Kenzie was referred to me by a friend after asking her if she had anyone amazing that she thought would be a good fit for this book. Within two weeks, I went from having never heard of Kenzie to interviewing her for the book and becoming a big supporter of her work. All we needed was a text intro and scheduling link via email to make it happen. Never underestimate the power of a great introduction.

What is the one thing that, if you knew when starting, would have accelerated your path to success?

The one thing would be taking smaller steps. I think I jumped so far that the past two years I've really had to go back and take a bunch of steps. I look at my fast-pace moving as a blessing and a curse because it's so beautiful, and I've accomplished so much and continue to accomplish a lot, but there's also a lot of turbulence I have created from taking massive steps. I've lost a lot of money, and it's definitely been a journey. And so, the one thing I would tell myself is to take smaller steps and let the journey lead you. For a while I was chasing the end result, and now I've learned that there is no end result; so, it's better off to just take bites of the cookie versus trying to eat the whole thing.

What are three pieces of software/technology you recommend people use in their business?

Google Drive

Lightroom

WhatsApp

Slack

For somebody who has dreams of being a wildly successful entrepreneur with freedom, what is the most important thing to focus on?

Embody your message. I think that's very, very important. When you embody your message and you embody what you're doing, that's when you see the most success. That's when things stick. That's when people understand your message. That's when people begin to trust you. Then it's sticking to your messages because when you get started in entrepreneurship and you start to see a little bit of money and you have an Instagram following, you will get persuaded in so many different directions. I did for a few months, and I had to come back to my center and my message because that is what's super important. I think nowadays, there's so many people out there, there's so many entrepreneurs, and what sets you apart is you and your unique business. So, you have to really embody your message and stand by it and not be persuaded by the outer world.

No entrepreneurial journey goes from A to B in a straight line. How did you overcome the internal doubts and external adversity along the journey?

They arise a lot. My first two years in the industry, I had absolutely no fear. I was balls to the walls. Then I developed some fear when I started to see different patterns in finances, and I started to invest more in my business, and I started to work on things in a more dedicated way because it started to mean more to me. Then with that, it's like the more you know, the more fear can creep in. It still arises all the time, so what I do to find my center and to eliminate those doubts is to really align with my core. Oftentimes when those arise, things become and seem very chaotic in my life as a whole, so it'll be coming back to the things that make me feel good like movement and meditating. Where's my environment? Where am I staying? I'm the first person to pick up and move. I travel. I'm really aware of my environment and the energy that's around me, and if I can align myself to my natural state, then I'm able to overcome anything.

It usually has nothing to do with the business, which is what we all blame things on at first—I'm not making enough money, or my developer's not on time—but then if I really think about it, it's all me. If I can get myself into a good, aligned state, then I can perform at my best, and I can see things more clearly. I just started praying a lot when I'm feeling fear before bed, and it helps. I think just connecting and trusting that there's something else out there that has us and supports us is super crucial because I'm so hard on myself and I will put everything on me, and that's a lot to carry. So, whenever I can surrender and give that power over to something greater, that's how I can overcome my fears.

What is your definition of success?

My definition of success is to feel empowered, to have your work and your life flowing through you (not resisting it), and to be embracing every single aspect of the journey and receiving what you put out. At times, I've wondered, "Why am I not receiving what I feel like I should," and I have to look at myself and ask, "Are you putting out what you should be getting back?" I believe if you put out quality, if you put out goodness into the world with intent, you will receive all that abundance back.

How do you relentlessly pursue excellence, greatness, and success (however you define it), while at the same time enjoy the journey of life?

I'm going to be so transparent. I'm still learning how to do that. My mantra this year is balance because I feel like in the past two years, I'm either all in in my career or trying to maintain or create my own personal life. I'm working on finding where that balance is, but to me, success is also that balance. It's that dance. It's that flow. I think that's real success and true happiness.

What is one action you recommend someone do every day to be the best version of themselves?

Starting your day off with a really beautiful, strong foundation. Maybe it's a nice fruit bowl, a couple rounds of breath work, moving your body, stretching, or having a nice cup of coffee, if you love that. I think that really lays the path for the rest of the day and the things that you do every single day or what makes your life up as a whole, so I find that the key to success is found in our tiny little rituals and daily routines.

How have relationships—personal and professional— contributed to your success and happiness?

Relationships have come and gone my entire life since I was born. I was born a child that was always in search of something else. I was in every kind of school system you could imagine. I always had new friends because I was on this quest as a young child for more. I always questioned the system. I always would sit in this class and think, "How will I use this in life? Is this important to know?" I just wanted to be in the world and doing things with my hands, and it was really, really tough to be a kid and a teenager in a world that really loves its systems and people that can fit in. So, friends have come and gone, but this past year, when I have become so super, super aligned in my career, in my message, in myself, in my soul, in me as a human, I am making the deepest, most long-lasting connections that match who I actually am, because I think, for the first time ever, I've really come into who I am, what my career is, and what my message is. It's not rocking like a boat anymore. It's solid, and it's growing into the ground, and I'm now attracting those same kinds of people. All my friends are huge entrepreneurs. They are into wellness. They're into spirituality. We have endless things to talk about. They make me better, and I make them better, and I find that when you are aligned with yourself—truly aligned—that's when those people that will stay come into your life.

Who are three of your favorite entrepreneurs to follow, learn from, and/or connect with?

Jesse Itzler

Heath Ellis

Peta Kelly

MIRROR, MIRROR ON THE WALL

Mirror. This was a word that stuck with me throughout all these interviews. Every time someone mentioned it, it hit home.

Whether it's a literal mirror and you're staring at yourself, or a figurative mirror triggered by an external person or situation, a mirror is often a tool for reflection.

I think we tend to avoid the mirror because it forces us to look at ourselves. As a society, we're great at calling out other people, but when it comes to ourselves, we like to think we have it all figured out—or we like to tell that to ourselves to avoid the uncomfortable.

Whether it was Ben Newman talking about how you should look in the mirror at the end of every day and be honest with yourself about whether or not you gave it your best today, or Rachel Bell discussing how her business development journey as an entrepreneur is a mirror for her personal development, or Serena Poon touching on how relationships are a mirror for what you need to work on, or Alexi Panos sharing how being a parent has been the biggest mirror for showing her all the places she wasn't showing up for herself or was being inauthentic, we can all agree that mirrors have a lot to say.

Mirrors are one of the few things that instantaneously cause us to think about our external appearance and our internal thoughts.

When we look at a mirror, there is nothing to look at but ourselves. For most of us, that's uncomfortable and often leads to negative self-talk or exploitation in certain areas of our life where we know we aren't living up to our true greatness.

I think we need to give ourselves permission to change the narrative. Instead of looking at a mirror and seeing it as an amplifier to our doubts, shortcomings, and insecurities, we can look at a mirror and see the opportunity within. The opportunity to grow, the opportunity to love, the opportunity to become who we are meant to become.

THE ELEVATED ENTREPRENEUR

When it comes to mirrors created by people or experiences, I think it's important to give ourselves grace and the permission to feel. When we feel and truly open up, we give ourselves the best chance to see, learn, and understand how to improve. And that's all life is. Doing the best we can to be the best we can in order to achieve the life we define as successful.

When I look into a mirror, there are always negative thoughts that come, and I know I'm not alone in this. Even for naturally positive people, we all have mirror thoughts that tend to be negative. "Look at that pimple, damn it." "Shit, another gray hair." "If only I had chiseled abs. Shouldn't have had that Taco Bell last night." "What am I doing?" "Who am I to build this thing/business?"

I was riding my Peloton, and after thirty minutes of kicking my butt, my friend Kendall Toole talked about how we need to give ourselves some love, and I loved that. Too often, we are our own harshest critic, and while that can be beneficial at times, we forget how powerful our thoughts and words can be.

We all have that mean voice inside our head that talks to us way more than we want it to. You know the voice I'm talking about.

Instead of letting it dictate the conversation, we need to take control of how we talk to ourselves and use that voice inside our head to lift us up not tear us down. Would you allow the voice inside your head to talk to your friends the way it does to you? I don't think so.

We all have flaws. We all have insecurities. We all have things that we can work on. But we are also all amazing in our own way. We have greatness within us, and when you feed your mind with the right thoughts and you talk to yourself with hype and love, things begin to change.

During my speaking events, I have entrepreneurs and people all over the world do an activity I call the Selfless Compliment. Here's how it works. It's incredibly awkward the first time yet incredibly powerful, and people love it.

The Selfless Compliment

Take out your phone and flip on the video camera.

Click the record button.

For twenty to thirty seconds, film yourself giving compliments to yourself. During this time, you can only hype yourself up.

Click stop and put your phone down.

Take a deep breath.

Some people tend to make it funny and say, "Damn, my eyebrows are looking good today!"

Some people take it super seriously: "I am powerful. I am strong. I am loved. I am an amazing friend."

There's no right way to do this other than to speak to yourself in a way that builds you up.

Every time I do this exercise, I ask if anyone felt uncomfortable. Almost immediately, everyone's hand goes up. Then I pause and tell them that while it might have been uncomfortable, every single person was smiling. There is incredible power when you use a mirror for growth and open yourself up to what's possible.

As much as mirrors can help us see within, mirrors can also be a way to amplify our greatness.

The Hype Up Meeting is one of the best ways I have found to encourage and support myself. Entrepreneurship can be lonely at times, and there are always going to be waves of emotions. The Hype Up Meeting can and will help you stay focused, clear, intentional, and of course, hyped to continue on your journey.

The Hype Up Meeting

Allocate a fifteen-minute time slot on your calendar weekly and title it "Hype Up Meeting." (Yes, actually put it in the calendar.)

Turn on your favorite music.

Stand in front of the mirror and get hyped. This may look like dancing your heart out with absolutely no fear, releasing all expectations, staring at yourself, positive self-talk, "I am" statements, or doing whatever you can think of to increase your energy and hype you up.

Finish with a deep breath.

My favorite part of the Hype Up Meeting is it's just me and myself. I tend to walk back and forth hyping myself up. I remind myself of why I do what I do. I sometimes even pretend I'm in an arena and I pump myself up by waving my arms up and down like I'm getting the crowd to go crazy. Most importantly, I let myself be fully in the moment without worrying about anyone or anything else.

Mirrors. Who would've thought I'd spend some time talking about something we've looked at every day of our lives? Tag me @jakekelfer on Instagram when you have your own Hype Up Meetings and Selfless Compliments!

AMANDA HOLMES

Bio

Amanda Holmes' singing career spanned over seven years and four records. When her father, Chet Holmes, NY Times best-selling author, was diagnosed with leukemia, it all came to an abrupt end. After studying alternative medicines in Asia under her guru, she inherited the responsibility of her father's business. Imagine you're twenty-four years old as a singer/songwriter, and now you have hundreds of staff all double your age, and you have to know what to do. Today, she has been the CEO of Chet Holmes International for many years now. CHI has assisted a quarter of a million businesses worldwide. Based on her father's teachings from, *The Ultimate Sales Machine,* his book has been voted in the top ten most recommended sales books of all time. She is dedicated to not only carrying on her father's legacy but, most of all, making a difference for business owners around the world.

How to Connect

IG: @ultimatesalesmachine

FB: /ultimatesalesmachine

Website: chetholmes.com

How We Met

I was scrolling through Instagram like we all do, and I kept coming across this person Amanda Holmes. After the fourth or fifth time, I decided that I needed to stop scrolling and meet her. So, instead of reaching out with no intention, I immediately added value and invited her to join the book as a great way to feature her story and spread her message while also building our relationship.

What is the one thing that, if you knew when starting, would have accelerated your path to success?

I inherited a company that had been in business for twenty years, and it just got plopped in front of me as my father passed, and there was no plan for me to take over the business. Never once did my father sit me down and show me all of the companies and how they run and what the products are. So here I am, twelve companies under my umbrella, and I see a P&L, and it just makes me cry because I had no idea how to run any of these companies. We were running very old systems, so my team and I had to rebuild every single freaking piece of it, from offline to bringing our first online sale. We really had to adapt to be able to sustain and flourish as we do now, so if I had to say one thing to myself it would be that you need to innovate.

What are three pieces of software/technology you recommend people use in their business?

ClickFunnels

Keap

Canva

For somebody who has dreams of being a wildly successful entrepreneur with freedom, what is the most important thing to focus on?

The first thing that comes up is time management. To be able to truly be free, you have to create something that's valuable. You can't just shortcut your way to that as much as the internet may want us to believe that you can be a success overnight.

I just interviewed Russell Brunson, and he did from zero to $100,000,000 in four years, but it took thirty years of learning how to do that to be able to have that success over four years. One of the crucial skill sets that the majority of people lose track of is time. A billionaire makes a billion dollars, and yet we have the same twenty-four hours in a day. Master your skill of time management, and you'll be able to go further faster.

What is your definition of success?

My definition of success is if at the end of the day I can put my head on my pillow and feel good about myself, then I'm successful. If something is off, and I have a hard time with that, then I know that there's something that needs to shift in my life. To me, the relationship that I have with myself is most important, and then everything else flows. If I'm passionate because I'm doing this thing and it's helping people or it's generating me wealth or it's giving me freedom, that's all great, but ultimately, everything just starts with me and myself.

How do you relentlessly pursue excellence, greatness, and success (however you define it), while at the same time enjoy the journey of life?

When I'm at my best, I let go of my own desires and pursuits and surrender myself to be a conduit of something greater. That is excellence in its purest form.

What is one action you recommend someone do every day to be the best version of themselves?

I would say tuning into yourself, however that looks. For me, I love playing music, so I chant. It could be meditating, journaling, walking, watching the sun rise, or taking long, deep breaths for three minutes right before you go to bed. It's just that process of looking within. It's something that I don't think a lot of people talk about, and I think that's what's missing. We're so focused on what everyone else thinks of us, rather than just tuning in and asking how I feel about myself.

How have relationships—personal and professional—contributed to your success and happiness?

They're huge. I have my father that I've studied under for business in the sense that when I inherited the company, I had to watch all of his training programs to learn just like everyone else because he had never formally taught me any of that. I'd never been to a seminar. I had never gone through any of his stuff, so he's a huge mentor for me.

Then I also have a spiritual mentor as well. Her name is Sarva Loka Maa Her Holiness Sri Sri Sri 1008 Guruji Poonamji, a.k.a. Guruji. It's a very long formal title, but she's been crucial to my evolution. I really believe that you need mentorship to get to places faster. Find somebody that's done it already, and then have them guide you.

Who are three of your favorite entrepreneurs to follow, learn from, and/or connect with?

Kari Warberg Block

Tom Douglas

Russell Brunson

TRAVIS CHAPPELL

Bio

Travis Chappell is the founder and CEO of Guestio, a new software that connects high-level guests with high-level content creators, and he is the host of the top-rated show, *Build Your Network*. In addition to being featured in *Entrepreneur, NASDAQ, Yahoo Finance,* and *ReadWrite,* Travis has also been featured in *Forbes* as a top ten podcast that will change your life alongside Joe Rogan, Gary Vaynerchuk, Tim Ferriss, and the like.

How to Connect

IG: @travischappell

FB Group: Podcast to Profit

Website: travischappell.com

How We Met

As a networking and people-loving person, when I saw Travis's podcast called *Build Your Network*, I knew we needed to be connected. I reached out to be on his show, and although it didn't work out right away, he still wanted to connect. I took him up on the offer, and we hit it off talking all things basketball. As I got to know more about Travis and his incredible work helping people create profitable podcasts, I knew he'd be a great fit, so I asked him if he wanted to be featured.

What is the one thing that, if you knew when starting, would have accelerated your path to success?

When I started a business in general, I wish I could go back and give myself the advice to learn online marketing sooner. In my early adulthood, I did door-to-door sales for six years. I don't necessarily regret that time because I learned a ton. I think it's like taking a crash course in emotional intelligence and in selling, and I think those skills have been really valuable in a lot of other things that I've been able to do, but I wish I would have started something online back then because I had so much free time, and I was making good money. So, it would have been the perfect time for me to start a podcast or start doing something online, gaining an audience, building an email list, doing something like that, but it was just not even on my radar. I wish I would have done that sooner.

One thing I wish I would have known when I started this current business (Guestio) in software is what a minimum viable product (MVP) really is and what it looks like. I was trying to come up with an MVP, and by the time I launched, I realized this is definitely not an MVP. This is way bulkier than an MVP needed to be, and I learned that the hard way. We had to scrap an entire feature set that we built out for the launch because people didn't respond well to it when we launched the product, and it was just like, "Oh, this is what they mean by minimum viable product." All you want to do is prove the concept first, that's it. It cost me tens of thousands of dollars, and it was more money than I needed to spend to be able to figure out the same exact thing that I figured out without having spent the money. I wish I would have had a more clear understanding of what it meant to test and prove a concept to a market and find that product market fit.

What are three pieces of software/technology you recommend people use in their business?

ClickUp

Zoom

Guestio

For somebody who has dreams of being a wildly successful entrepreneur with freedom, what is the most important thing to focus on?

Invest in yourself from the beginning. There's so much to learn, so get in and start learning ASAP. If you're just getting started in business, start learning for free at first. Take some free courses, watch YouTube, listen to podcasts, and then start getting some books, listen to some audio books, and then start investing in yourself. Hire a coach, hire a mentor, get into a mastermind, or join something where you can get around a bunch of other people. I think your focus should be on knowledge, and your focus should be on your network. You should be focusing on filling your circle with a bunch of other people who are a lot more successful than you and then a bunch of other people who are a little bit more successful than you. You want people who are a year or two ahead of you on the journey and then people who are twenty years ahead of you, people who have astronomical success.

If you want a tactical answer, sales is the tactical answer. If you have already started a business and you need to get it going or you're not going to pay the bills next month, then you better get pretty good at selling. I mentioned earlier that I wish I was better at marketing when I first started in all this, and that's definitely the case. But I'm happy that I was good with selling because marketing costs money, selling makes money.

What is your definition of success?

Self-awareness. I think success is defined differently for everybody, so you really have to ask that question to yourself, and you have to be okay with the definition. The only caveat here is you are not allowed to convince yourself that your current life is success because chances are, it's not, and you're probably just saying that because your mind is probably convincing you that that's the case because you are afraid of the amount of work that you might have to do in order to actually achieve the version of success that you think you are capable of. Get crystal clear and get self-aware. What does success mean for me? What do I want out of my life? For me, success is having freedom, having money, and being able to spend time with those that I love. Those are the big things for me.

What is one action you recommend someone do every day to be the best version of themselves?

Exercise.

How have relationships—personal and professional— contributed to your success and happiness?

They're everything. I know I kind of beat a dead horse all the time talking about networking and relationships and how life changing they are, but it's just true. When I started all of this, I came out of a really tight-knit religious bubble background, and when I left that world, I was pretty much starting from scratch in terms of my network, especially a professional network. I didn't know anybody in business, let alone anybody that was successful in business, and so I was literally starting from scratch, and I think that's probably why it matters so much to me. I didn't start my network with I had a friend in college whose dad was super rich, mentored me on a daily basis, and introduced me to his golf buddies. It was something that I had to get super purposeful about if I wanted to make it happen because it wasn't going to happen by accident. I had to make it happen on purpose, and so that's probably why it means so much to me. There is this interesting book from Ben Hardy called *Willpower Doesn't Work,* and there is a study about how even if you know you're doing things incorrectly in life and you want to change them, willpower is not enough to change them. The only thing that really changes them is your environment, and one of the biggest aspects of your environment is the people that you hang out with. If you really want to change, if you truly desire to make yourself a better version of yourself, then do the one thing that you have control over, which is change your environment and change the people that you're hanging around with all the time.

I'm not one of those people that's like, screw all your friends from high school. They don't deserve you. I'm not that kind of a person. I still hang out with all my friends on occasion, but you have to—on purpose—spend time with people who may not be in your current friend circle who will push you to be a better version of yourself in whatever aspect it might be in. Get a gym partner that goes to the gym every day, and that way you're staying accountable to them to go into the gym. Get in a small mastermind group where you do weekly calls with people that are making progress in their business from week to week and see how you can help them and how they can help you. Create an environment that is most conducive for you to be successful in and a huge part of that is relationships. Relationships have the ability to impact your life in a really, really positive way and in a really, really negative way, so if you haven't taken an audit or taken a step back and asked yourself, "Who are the five people in my life I spend the most time with and how can I make that be a group of people that push me to be a better version of myself?" I think it's time to do that and then see how you can work to get around more of the types of people that are going to push you to be a better version of who you are. Sometimes, it seems difficult and hard when you're going through it, but five years down the road from now, you'll be thanking yourself for taking actions like that today.

Who are three of your favorite entrepreneurs to follow, learn from, and/or connect with?

Tom Bilyeu

Elon Musk

Jesse Itzler

Sara Blakely

ALLIE CASAZZA

Bio

Allie Casazza is the host of *The Purpose Show*—a top-rated podcast—and the creator of online courses that have earned her international attention for her fresh, practical lifestyle strategies for moms. Known as "The Life Minimalist," she encourages and inspires women to pursue abundant life by creating space for what matters most. Allie and her husband, Brian, live with their four young children in Southern California wine country.

How to Connect

IG: @allie_thatsme
FB: /alliecasazzablog
Website: alliecasazza.com

How We Met

Allie and I met through a simple email introduction. Because the intro came from someone she trusts and respects, it was an easy yes. One email later, and we booked a call. One week after that, and we were in the Zoom room chatting it up.

What is the one thing that, if you knew when starting, would have accelerated your path to success?

Knowing that passive digital products where I can speak in and show myself on video and really engage with people in that way was the right path for me. I first started out with e-books and self-publishing digital books, and I thought that that book was going to be my big break and I would see hundreds of thousands of dollars. I thought, "This is it," but I didn't even make enough to pay the utility bill. It was so embarrassing, and it sucked, but those flops led me to try again and figure out what sticks, and then I landed on courses and programs and just fell in love. I wish I would have done them a little bit sooner.

What are three pieces of software/technology you recommend people use in their business?

Asana

Trello

Google Docs

For somebody who has dreams of being a wildly successful entrepreneur with freedom, what is the most important thing to focus on?

The most important thing is doing what feels really good in terms of delivering on the promises you're selling. I see a lot of people doing what other people are doing. Oh, they're doing courses, I'm going to do courses. What if you hate courses? What if you are an extrovert? What if you need that one-on-one, and you're really suited for coaching? I'm the opposite, coaching is not my vibe, but I found that when I feel really good about what's coming after the launch, after the delivery, my energy is higher. I'm way more likely to enroll more people, and I'm super excited. People can feel that. Everything really, really, really is energy, so starting at the base, what feels the highest vibe, what feels super good, and then align your business around that. Don't go and chase the dollar and step outside of what feels good to you just to make money and see what works. Align yourself first with what feels good, and then go from there.

No entrepreneurial journey goes from A to B in a straight line. How did you overcome the internal doubts and external adversity along the journey?

Honestly, it is grit. Just not stopping. I had three toddlers and a baby that was still nursing and not sleeping at night, and my husband was working his butt off for no money all day and all night. He was always gone, and it was just me and the babies chugging along and getting it done. I had this fifty-dollar laptop that I got from this creepy guy on Craigslist that barely worked. I would get up at ten till four every morning for a year working on my business, and honestly, it was so hard, and there were so many perceived failures, but I was on fire. I was so lit up. It was one of the best times of my life starting what is now this big empire. I feel like you have to hold the vision of what you know is coming because you decide if it's going to be that or if it's never going to be that. In my mind, there was no doubt that it wouldn't happen. It was just "Dang, this is taking a long time." It was the time; it wasn't the actual end result that I wasn't going to get there.

I heard this proverb when I was a kid that really stuck with me, and it says, "Where there is no vision, the people perish." If you have a vision for where you're going, it's like spotting for a dancer when she's twirling. If you know where you're going and you see that spot on the wall, no matter how flailing her arms get, you're going to hit that spot. With my story and how poor we were from the food bank stuff to cars getting repossessed and the repo guy banging on our door and hiding in the laundry room with the kids, it was so dramatic and hard. That vision was all I had, so I just gripped it tight and didn't let it go until it was my reality.

What is your definition of success?

Having the freedom to do whatever I want each day. Finances not depending on what I'm actually doing in the day-to-day. That pressure was on me for so long, and I just knew that's the first thing I wanted to change. I know money gives you options and freedom, and once I had those options and freedom, I really wanted to create a life where I could go for walks with my kids and sit and read or do whatever I wanted and not feel like "If I don't get this done today, then the money is not going to come, and I'm screwed." I feel like once I hit that and had options and freedom, that was success for me.

Most people never get started. What would you say to someone who has a dream but is holding back from making the plunge?

I think fear is a big flag waving at you and telling you this is what you need to pay attention to, and this is where you need to run toward. I found that when I opened my arms up to fear and really embraced it and treated it like the friend it actually is, I learned so much. When you are crap-your-pants terrified to do something, it is usually the way to go. What can I learn from this? How can I jump into this headfirst and just go all in, balls to the wall? Commit to saying, "I'm in, I'm going to win this." How can I just get to the next level? It's always through fear, so I feel like fear is the worst excuse to not start something.

How do you relentlessly pursue excellence, greatness, and success (however you define it), while at the same time enjoy the journey of life?

The things that I'm going for right now are things that would really freak a lot of people out. It's work and I work hard and I'm exhausted and I collapse at the end of the day, but at the same time, there's so much ease and flow.

I really think it's a state of mind. I think that you can choose to be in an inner state where you understand it gets to be good. The work I'm doing is good. It's a lot of hours sometimes, and it's a lot of energy, but it's good work, and it's beautiful. Sometimes it feels holy, it's just so good. Rest when you need to rest, but I think you can also choose to be productive from a place of ease, and that's something that I teach often. Change the scenery, change how you do a task, delegate or delete what you can, but when it comes down to really doing the thing, ask yourself, "How would it feel really good to do this?" Honestly, I record my podcast out of my spa all the time. It doesn't feel like work when you're just chatting out into thin air in your jacuzzi. It's joy.

I feel like we overcomplicate so much and punish ourselves in the way that we work so that we feel like we earned it when we get to what we're working for, and let me tell you, you already earned it. You are worthy because you are, so just do the work in a way that feels really, really good and enjoyable.

What is one action you recommend someone do every day to be the best version of themselves?

Every day, I get outside, and I start the day with taking care of myself: the sun on my face, going for a walk, getting my energy up, getting into gratitude. Getting outside, having the sunshine on me, being so grateful, and setting the intention is everything because we get to decide how it goes. Just deciding that today is going to be a good day, even if there's something on the calendar I don't feel like doing, is a chance for me to choose to reframe it. I wake up slow, but everyone seems to wake up really slow and decide that the day is going to be a shit show before it even has a chance to be anything. I just choose to see it positively, and I choose to get my energy going and set the intention. I get to decide how it goes.

How have relationships—personal and professional—contributed to your success and happiness?

I am married to a man who deeply supports me. I actually came from an extremely oppressive religious school that I went to growing up. They literally split up the boys and the girls, and the girls were taught how to wake up in the middle of the night and breastfeed and make meals, and the boys were taught how to balance checkbooks and start businesses. For me, in my marriage that needed to switch. I always say my husband was a feminist and a supporter before I even was. He cheered for me the whole time when I was like, "Hey, I need you to quit your job, and I know I haven't made any money yet, but I want the kids to be with a parent. And I need to start this business, and it's taking a lot." He quit, and he came home with donuts, and was like, "I quit. Good luck. I'm here for you." Three terrifying months later, I did it. I did it because he was there. I think having a partner that supports you is absolutely a non-negotiable in my book.

I also think that when you start being successful, friends start to drop like flies. Everyone is supportive of you when you're small and cute, but when you start to make more money than your doctor and lawyer combined, people get weird real fast. I think you have to let them go. It's part of the ride. Surround yourself with people who are actually challenging you, that push you to do more, and that are legitimately happy for you when you win.

Who are three of your favorite entrepreneurs to follow, learn from, and/or connect with?

Chris Harder

Jill Stanton

Amanda Frances

STEVE J. LARSEN

Bio

For two years, Steve J. Larsen was the lead funnel builder at ClickFunnels for Russell Brunson, making a name for himself in the internet marketing world.

Eventually, Steve left to start his own company. Just thirteen months later, he went on to score his own Two Comma Club Award when his business crossed one million dollars. Seven months later, he earned his next million dollars, followed by another million in one day!

He has four highly successful podcasts, including *Sales Funnel Radio* and *Launch for Profit*, which teach the finer points of marketing, offer creation, and—most importantly—Internet cashflow strategies.

Steve is passionate about improving the economic confidence of entrepreneurs through capitalism. Steve and his team do their part by helping entrepreneurs design and launch wildly lucrative offers online.

How to Connect

Website: stevejlarsen.com

How We Met

I first heard of Steve when I took the One Funnel Away Challenge with ClickFunnels. Steve had some of the biggest energy I've ever seen, and I immediately gravitated to him. When I went to write this book, I thought he'd be a great guest, but since I had no personal connection to him, I submitted a general form on his website. Sure enough, right as I was about to wind down interviews, I received an email from his team asking to schedule our interview. I responded immediately and made sure I had space open to make this happen.

What is the one thing that, if you knew when starting, would have accelerated your path to success?

My product idea didn't really matter, and I needed to focus on the market more. I had someone tell me my idea was cool, but can you match that idea to a problem that's being had in the marketplace? If I just first started with who I wanted to sell to and what problem I wanted to solve rather than if I have a good idea, it would have easily short cut the first thirty-four product tries over five years. It took a long time for me to have a success story, and I would say that it would have at least chopped it in half.

What are three pieces of software/technology you recommend people use in their business?

ClickFunnels

Facebook

Email provider

For somebody who has dreams of being a wildly successful entrepreneur with freedom, what is the most important thing to focus on?

It's not the freedom. That comes way down the road. You have to build a business that replaces you. I'd say the biggest thing to focus on is learning how to say no. When you're starving as a brand-new entrepreneur and you need an opportunity, it's easy to say yes to everything because you just want something to work. What I wish someone had said to me is "Think through your vision, and if someone else is doing it, it means you can too, so say no to everything else." Being able to say no is big.

What is your definition of success?

In two ways. The first is the science of achievement. Did I get the outcome? That's very destination based. You have to sprint to it. You either got it or you didn't. You got the buck, or you didn't get the buck and you're still broke. Then there is the art of fulfillment, and it's a completely different game that I was not aware of. I was trying to play the art of fulfillment game with the science of achievement tools. I did not realize that they're not at all related. It's like playing football on a baseball field. It's not even relatable at all.

Most people never get started. What would you say to someone who has a dream but is holding back from making the plunge?

No one is going to give you permission. Eventually you need to carve your own path. If someone has the formula but isn't executing, I would say a few things. First, no one is going to give you permission. Second of all, in Tim Ferriss's *The 4 Hour Workweek,* he talks about how if something is pure hell, we do something about it. If we are in the thick of it, we find a way to exit or move. Anything short of pure hell, we figure out a way to compensate, so what it's really about is figuring out how you cannot tolerate the outskirts of pure hell and decide you want to change. No one is going to give you permission, and no one's coming to save you.

The competition is less than you think it is, and the chances of you succeeding are higher than you probably think it is, especially with the right formulas.

How do you relentlessly pursue excellence, greatness, and success (however you define it), while at the same time enjoy the journey of life?

About six months into working for Russell at ClickFunnels, he handed me a little mini course called The Gap. The reason he did it is because he looked at me and he told me, I see you seeing that guy over there doing things that you wish you could go do right now. He's like, "First of all, I appreciate you taking the time to be here at ClickFunnels and help me with this. Second of all, you have to stop comparing yourself to other people." You have to stop comparing yourself to other people in their timelines, and that's why my focus is, "It's me against me, and it's me against yesterday." Those blinders make it so I can pursue both those outcomes without self-judgment and more self-awareness. Learning how to meditate, lots of therapy, and self-work have been huge. I have to have an active plan for the art of fulfillment because no plan is a terrible plan. I certainly have plans for business, but if there's not a plan for how you're going to get fulfilled and discover what fulfills you, you're probably not going to be happy.

What is one action you recommend someone do every day to be the best version of themselves?

I love the quote, "We are what we repeatedly do." If you can consistently show up, you'll find out really quickly. Don't look at the clock, but six months will go by, and you'll realize how much you've grown. Then you'll do it again and see that you're starting to get way better than the rest of the market at your thing. I think it's just about showing up. Most people are so afraid that they're going to fail that they don't try anything, so you actually find that competition is so small. If you do anything, the chances of you succeeding are really high because most won't do anything.

How have relationships—personal and professional—contributed to your success and happiness?

You realize that it is the reason all along. It's all about relationships. I heard that when I was brand-new, and I was like "gag me." That's what I thought, but it's true. It's about relationships. There's a lot of lonely, rich people out there. You leave the art of fulfillment game behind when you leave relationships behind and burn bridges for the sake of the dollar.

Who are three of your favorite entrepreneurs to follow, learn from, and/or connect with?

Russell Brunson

Frank Kern

Roland Frasier

TYLER J. MCCALL

Bio

Tyler J. McCall is a business and Instagram marketing strategist for online business owners and digital entrepreneurs. He focuses on using Instagram and social media to tell stories, build relationships, and convert followers to fans, drawing from his ten years of experience in non-profit marketing and community organizing. Since 2015, Tyler has taught thousands of entrepreneurs how to start, grow, and scale their online businesses. He is the founder of the Follower to Fan Society—an online Instagram marketing training program—and of the Online Business Association—the first and only professional association for online business owners and digital entrepreneurs. Tyler is based in Asheville, North Carolina, where he lives with his husband, Eric. When he's not coaching or teaching, Tyler enjoys Target runs and road trips . . . that he documents on his Instagram Stories.

How to Connect

IG: @tylerjmccall

FB: /tylerjmccall

Website: tylerjmccall.com

How We Met

I first came across Tyler's stuff on Instagram after hearing him on Amy Porterfield's podcast. After doing what I call Podcast Tag, I shot Tyler a video DM introducing myself and sharing my favorite takeaway from the episode he did. Over the course of the next few months, I shared his content, listened to his podcast, and asked him questions about his journey. About four months after our first DM, I invited him to participate in the book as one of the featured guests. Fast forward three more months, and we made it happen.

What is the one thing that, if you knew when starting, would have accelerated your path to success?

Patience is going to be your greatest virtue on this journey. I think the way that comes up for me is that all the people you're following, you love, and you're obsessed with, and you're thinking, "My business is going to be like theirs one day," they started five years ago. Put in the time and pay your dues. Success can happen maybe more quickly than you think it can, but you have to be patient because it's going to take some time.

What are three pieces of software/technology you recommend people use in their business?

Monday.com

Slack

News Feed Eradicator Facebook Chrome plug-in

For somebody who has dreams of being a wildly successful entrepreneur with freedom, what is the most important thing to focus on?

The most important thing is creating a streamlined, scalable offer that you can easily explain to people, that you can easily sell, and that you can easily deliver. I know that this will take time, but work on removing yourself from as much of that product as possible outside of the forward-facing promotional stuff and then the inside supporting your client stuff. Everything else, you don't need to do. Focus on building out a team or support or a process or system—whatever you need to do to streamline that. That's been the key to my success, and I know that's been the key to so many others' success. I think a big part that we talk about but don't necessarily want to think about is that you have to do one thing. I know we want to do all of the things because we're creative and innovative and we have all the ideas to solve all the problems in the world, but just solve one problem right now. When you get really good at solving that problem and get really good at making a ton of money from solving that problem, then you can move on to the next one.

No entrepreneurial journey goes from A to B in a straight line. How did you overcome the internal doubts and external adversity along the journey?

I think having a community of people who you consider your peers is incredibly important. For me, having a solid group of half a dozen people who are right where I am in business, who are just behind where I am, or who are just ahead of where I am has been the biggest game changer for me. I think having that core group of people right there with you is going to be the biggest difference. If you're in a relationship with someone, make sure they're in it with you to have those conversations, because at the end of the day, when everything kind of falls away, that's all you have. That's the only person that you have when everything else is gone, so have those conversations with them and make sure they're in it with you. The biggest thing is being crystal clear on why you're doing all of this and having a super clear vision, so when you wake up in the morning and you're not feeling it that day or when you don't want to get on video or when you really just want to keep scrolling, you know what you're working towards and always go back to that.

What is your definition of success?

Success for me is having the impact I want while making the income that I want, and while having the freedom and spaciousness in my life that I want. Freedom and spaciousness are key. That's the thing that I'm always asking myself: "Is this in line with the freedom that I want?" For me, when I think of spaciousness, I'm always thinking of openness, freedom, and breathing room. Does it serve that and, at the same time, create impact and create income that I want? Where that kind of trifecta meets is where the magic happens.

Most people never get started. What would you say to someone who has a dream but is holding back from making the plunge?

Start by making one decision, just one simple decision, and know that is the domino that's going to help you make those next decisions. I love the idea of how you eat an elephant—one bite at a time—so that's how you build a business. One decision at a time.

I have a little framework that I teach that has helped me with making decisions. The first part is to get really clear on whose vision you're channeling and making the decision. Is it your vision or is it someone else's vision? You want to make sure that it's in line with what you want. The second thing is to get really clear on what that decision is going to cost you, and knowing that whenever you make a decision, it can cost something, and it's not always money. It could cost you time, your reputation, resources, or whatever it may be. The third question is just asking yourself, "Is it worth it?" Whenever you're feeling like you're stuck in indecision, tell yourself, "Okay, I'm going to make a decision. I'm going to ask myself these three questions, and I'm going to decide, and then I'm not going to think about that decision anymore." Then just execute step by step by step.

How do you relentlessly pursue excellence, greatness, and success (however you define it), while at the same time enjoy the journey of life?

For me, when I'm on, I'm on, and when I'm off, I'm off. It's so corny, but it is very work hard, play hard, which I totally identify with. It works well for me. When I'm in my office at home, when I'm working, I'm here, I'm dialed in, no distraction, nothing getting in my way. When that clock hits four p.m., I am on the couch, I'm scrolling Twitter, I'm watching YouTube with my husband, we're trying to figure out what we're going to order from GrubHub for dinner, and I'm just hanging out. I'm not worried about business when I'm living my life, and I also know that when I'm in my business, when I'm working, I'm going to do it on my terms.

I set my day the way I want. I work the hours I want. As a company policy that I made up, we have all these days off every year, and we always have a three-day weekend. We don't work on Fridays because who the heck wants to work on Fridays. Literally no one. I set my life up that way intentionally, so when I'm working, I'm working, and when I'm off, I'm off. And that way, I can accomplish my goals and then have a lot of freedom in my life too.

What is one action you recommend someone do every day to be the best version of themselves?

Put pen to paper in some way. I think that tactical experience is so important, and we've lost that with technology. Whether that's outlining your to-do list for the day, putting everything from your calendar into a planner, writing a gratitude list, or writing in a journal, I'd say to put pen to paper in some way every day.

How have relationships—personal and professional—contributed to your success and happiness?

I honestly wouldn't, and I don't say this lightly. I would not be here today if it were not for relationships in my life. I've had a tough journey in a number of ways (mental health, navigating depression and grief, post-traumatic stress disorder, and also being a queer man), so, for me, those relationships have been so key. Having people that I can go to when I feel like I'm low and I need the support or the people to cheer me on has been huge. I'm a competitive person, so having people that I can compete against in my mind is so key for me. Another thing is remembering that my ideas aren't as good as I think they are and that I need people to poke holes in my ideas. I think so much of successful entrepreneurship is just stripping away ego and getting out of your own way. I always say I'm a recovering know-it-all. One of the biggest things I had to learn to be successful is that I don't know everything, and I think having community is key because you need people to poke holes in your ideas, because the only way you can create better ideas is by people ripping apart the ideas you have right now.

Who are three of your favorite entrepreneurs to follow, learn from, and/or connect with?

Rachel Rodgers

Jereshia Hawk

Paul Fishman

JESS GLAZER

Bio

A former celebrity personal trainer and elementary school teacher, Jess turned her once "cute side hustle" into a multimillion-dollar business in two years.

Since leaving her teaching job in 2017, she has hired a team of incredible heart-centered leaders, served hundreds of clients, and helped create over seven million dollars in revenue for those clients (in under two years). During the 2020 global pandemic, Jess and her team were able to help seven new entrepreneurs create million-dollar businesses from the ground up; she is committed to helping ninety-three more!

As a result of donations/awareness, she and her husband built a school in Ghana, Africa, with Pencils of Promise. The doors officially opened in January 2021.

She's been featured in *The Wall Street Journal, Forbes, Yahoo Finance, The Today Show, Good Day New York, The New York Post, Shape* magazine, and *Well + Good.*

Her mission is to cause a ripple effect and inspire change for generations to come, making a massive impact and leaving a lasting legacy beyond her singular actions.

How to Connect

IG: @jessglazer

How We Met

It all started when I was on a podcast called *The Art of Masculinity* hosted by Johnny Elsasser. After the podcast, I filled him in on my book and what I was working on. Shortly after, I saw him hanging with Jess via an IG Story and knew I had to meet Jess. I hit Johnny up and asked if he would be willing to connect us. Being the great dude he is, he made the intro via Instagram DMs. After a few months of going back and forth with Jess in DMs, we made the interview happen, and since then, she's played a huge role in my growth as an entrepreneur.

What is the one thing that, if you knew when starting, would have accelerated your path to success?

There are so many pieces to this, but part of it is asking for help, which goes hand in hand with investing. It's one of those not-so-sexy answers because everybody uses it, but truly it would have accelerated my business if I asked for help sooner and I left my ego at the door and said, "Hey, I don't know something. Can you help me?"

What are three pieces of software/technology you recommend people use in their business?

Zoom or Skype for video calls

Kajabi

The social media platform your ideal client is hanging out on

For somebody who has dreams of being a wildly successful entrepreneur with freedom, what is the most important thing to focus on?

Impact. I don't even have to think twice about that answer. If you're focused on the what and the why and the when, you're doing it all wrong. If you focus on the impact of what it is that you're doing and how you are serving, it becomes effortless and it starts to get really easy. Not to say that it is an easy job or that it doesn't take a lot of work. It definitely requires work, but it becomes effortless because when you're just serving, when you're showing up and making an impact, the income will come and the freedom will come.

No entrepreneurial journey goes from A to B in a straight line. How did you overcome the internal doubts and external adversity along the journey?

I don't think I've overcome it. It's something I struggle with daily. I still honestly have to unfollow people. I find myself muting competitors or peers, even clients and friends in this space that trigger me.

I don't really think imposter syndrome is really a syndrome. I think we all feel like imposters sometimes, and we all have it, so therefore, I don't really think of it as a syndrome. There's nothing wrong with us. Feeling like a fraud, feeling like an imposter, feeling as if we aren't good enough, or whatever that might be are all things that I still struggle with every day, and like they say, new levels, new devils. They'll come up in different iterations whether it's realizing I'm leading of team of eleven and asking how did that happen. I went from solopreneur to all of a sudden entrepreneur, and sometimes, I forget that I'm a leader and I'm leading a team of eleven and people are looking to me for guidance while I'm in my RV in my sweats, and sometimes I can't believe this is my job.

I think doing a lot of the internal work—asking yourself deeper questions, finding incredible support, surrounding yourself with like-minded people who are going through what you're going through—are all things that have helped me over the years. Also, time inconsistencies. Something I am very, very transparent about is there is a very sexy story that I've built this multi-seven-figure business in under three years. That's sexy, right? But that's not what happened. When I really zoom out and look at when I started this "cute side hustle" and when I was throwing spaghetti at a wall and trying e-books and blogging and all these different things, that was eight years ago. It certainly has not been an overnight success.

What is your definition of success?

That has changed a lot over the years. It definitely used to be more vanity metrics of financials. I wouldn't call it fame but having that credibility. I came from the fitness world, and I've been a celebrity personal trainer for seventeen years, so it was all about magazine covers and eight-page spreads, and that meant a lot to me. The external permission, validation, recognition used to be my definition of success. As I've gotten older and as I handled and dealt with burnout twice and some other health issues, success now is feeling in alignment, feeling lit up and excited, having purpose, and having passion behind my purpose.

Most people never get started. What would you say to someone who has a dream but is holding back from making the plunge?

It's really easy to say just do it or just start. It's really easy to say that, but I think what it really requires is a reframe and that we go back to that impact and service mentality. Without being too dramatic, who are you robbing by not sharing your gifts? You're actually stealing from somebody. You're stealing opportunities and solutions. If you have solutions to problems, you could have a business. You don't have to have a business, but you could. So, if you have a solution to a problem and you're not willing to share that with people, then you're stealing from them. You're robbing them of that experience.

How do you relentlessly pursue excellence, greatness, and success (however you define it), while at the same time enjoy the journey of life?

I surround myself with people who keep me in check. I surround myself with people who call me out on my BS. I have little litmus tests for myself along the way, checking in whether it's weekly, monthly, quarterly.

I'll give myself a scorecard as the CEO of a company. I'll give everybody else scorecards as well. Everybody gets tested on things. We monitor everybody's tasks and what they're doing for the company. I do the same thing with myself, and sometimes, I need a coach to hold me accountable or a friend or my husband. I check in with myself, and I check in most importantly with my husband, my immediate circle, my closest friends, and my parents. I'll ask how I'm doing as a daughter, and the answers don't always feel good. You have to remember that feedback is neutral, and when you're coming from a place of compassion and wanting to grow, it's okay if it stings a little bit. "The last couple months I haven't been the best at fill-in-the-blank"—taking care of myself, calling my parents, whatever that is—and now it's about making a change and adjusting moving forward.

What is one action you recommend someone do every day to be the best version of themselves?

Something that has changed my life has been meditating. Meditating, breathwork, and just sitting still. I can't give you a definition of the perfect morning routine or what millionaires do to start their day. It has to be what works for you, and you really need to figure out and ask yourself, what do I need today? Sometimes, it's a high intensity workout, or sometimes, it's sleeping an extra ten minutes. It's learning to tune into that gut intuition of what do I need today to show up to be the best version of myself for my clients and other people.

How have relationships—personal and professional—contributed to your success and happiness?

They're everything. People say your network is your net worth. Relationships are everything, and I want to be clear here, it's not just about the entrepreneur, the coach, the person who's ahead of you, but it's also just the people that are around you, and, for lack of a better term, the people that you feel are behind you. Those people that you feel are behind you still serve a purpose in your life, and it's up to you to start to delineate and distinguish what is the purpose and role that all of these people play in my life. If you look at your life like a movie, there's different actors and actresses, and they play different roles. We have supporting people, we have key people, and we have the background people at the coffee shop. When you know and you have an intention and an understanding for the roles that people play, you can go into those times that you spend with them with more intention.

For me, there was a time six, seven years ago I got really frustrated with a lot of my high school and college friends because they weren't coming with me. They weren't on the entrepreneurial, professional development, Tony Robbins bandwagon I was on, so I used to get frustrated with them that they weren't meeting me where I was, but rather, it was my fault. I should be meeting them where they're at and not expecting them to come or expecting them to be excited or expecting them to want to talk about these things. Now, if I go into a weekend of hanging out with those friends, almost ten years later, I know that the container of the weekend is glory days and memories and fun high school Jess, and that's great because that fills my cup and it fills my soul and it's really good and I love them. I love them, but they're not the people I'm going to talk about landing pages and funnels with, and that's okay.

I think relationships have been everything. Knowing that everyone comes into your life for a reason and not everyone has to be in your life forever is important. Everybody comes in to teach us something, and sometimes what they teach stings, and sometimes those relationships end and that's okay. You can move on from that, and you also don't have to cut friends off left and right as you grow.

Who are three of your favorite entrepreneurs to follow, learn from, and/or connect with?

James Wedmore

Chris Harder

Lori Harder

Tony Robbins

Lewis Howes

THE ONE THING WE ALL SEEK: FREEDOM!

That is what we all seek. Every entrepreneur and coach I talk to tells me they want freedom. That is the desired result most people want.

When you break this down, freedom is the end result because we associate fulfillment and happiness with freedom. We associate these because when we have freedom, we have the power to choose.

Choose what we do with money.

Choose what we do with our time.

Choose where we spend our time.

Choose who we spend our time with.

Freedom creates an opportunity for us to take control of our time.

And what is time?

Time is the one thing we all want more of, yet it's one of the things we can never get back. It also happens to be one of the things we are worst at protecting and using.

Most of the world gives their time freely and then complains about not having time to do what they want, finish their tasks, spend time nourishing their most important relationships, or build the business they want.

Would you throw one hundred dollars in the garbage just for shits and giggles? Probably not. Yet, most of us dispose of time this exact way, inevitably delaying our ability to create the success and freedom we desire.

I used to have a terrible relationship with money, but as I continue to go on my own journey, I've realized making more money is an accelerator to freedom. Does money solve all my problems? Absolutely not. But does it allow me to make different choices? 100%. Making more money means I'm impacting more people. It means I can give more. It means I can provide more jobs. It means I can create experiences for others.

So, when we look at becoming a wildly successful entrepreneur with freedom, the Elevated Entrepreneur gets laser-focused on the things that actually matter.

We define success and get clear on what we truly want to achieve and who we want to be.

We set massive goals that are attainable.

We invest in ourselves.

We understand our numbers and what it's going to take to get there.

We create structure and systems to free up time.

We get focused on solving a single problem for a specific group of people.

We embrace the seasons of life.

We remember our why every day because purpose is stronger than passion.

We focus on experiences and creating memories and not just making a shit ton of money.

We make choices based on our highest selves.

We embrace sales and invite people to join us.

We focus on the people who matter most to us and spend time with them consistently.

We show up and do what we say we are going to.

We make an impact.

Freedom is available to us all! It's not an either-or option. You can have it all!

SYDNEY WEBB

Bio

As the founder and CEO of Toto, the world's first superfood cookie dough company, Sydney is a woman making major change in the world of health, wellness, and the food system at large. After being diagnosed with colon cancer at twenty-one and healing herself completely holistically, Sydney set out to share her experience with the world in a delicious way that no one could resist, and alas, Toto was born. Today, Sydney continues to inspire people with her story and change people's lives by changing what's on their plate.

How to Connect

IG: @sydneyoliviaaah & @totofoods

Website: toto.co

How We Met

Sydney and I met through Steve O'Dell, and we've become great friends. I absolutely love her story and company, so I asked her to be part of this book.

What is the one thing that, if you knew when starting, would have accelerated your path to success?

It's so funny because I actually reflect on this often. I think the biggest lesson that I'm still learning now is that it is not only okay but recommended that you ask for help. I think that, in the beginning especially, I was really intimidated by how much I didn't know, and I think now, the further along I've gone on my journey, the more humble I am every day. I think you have to be really comfortable with getting outside of your comfort zone and asking people, because not only does that accelerate your learning process so much faster, but you realize it really does take a village and it builds an amazing network of people who want to help you. People are so generous and more than willing to share their knowledge, so I think utilizing that is key.

What are three pieces of software/technology you recommend people use in their business?

Airtable

Slack

Google Sheets

For somebody who has dreams of being a wildly successful entrepreneur with freedom, what is the most important thing to focus on?

I think the most important thing to focus on is truly paying attention to the things that matter most to you. I went pedal to the medal the first couple of years, and it was totally necessary, and I think now, finding that balance and really homing in on your why every single day has been crucial for me. As someone on a mission who really wants to change the world of health, wellness, food, etc., there's a really big disconnect sometimes from that dream and checking off tasks on a Google sheet. It doesn't feel like it in the moment, so I spend time every morning connecting to that and thinking about the bigger picture because the why is everything. It's not my quote, but a quote that I think of often is, "When you know your why, you can bear almost any how." And I just think it's so powerful because it's true.

No entrepreneurial journey goes from A to B in a straight line. How did you overcome the internal doubts and external adversity along the journey?

Remember why you're doing it in the first place. I read a lot of stories about other entrepreneurs, and I'm fascinated by their stories because most of the most successful companies in the world have never been on this straight up incline. It's a rollercoaster for so many people, and what I think of often is it's not over until you quit, and you're the only one that's in control of that. It's totally natural for things to be great some days and not so great others. It's part of the learning process, and I never consider anything a failure. I just consider it a learning opportunity.

What is your definition of success?

The biggest thing for me has been creating a life that I'm proud to live both externally and internally, and the more I've focused and homed in on things that matter to me internally, the more I'm able to give. I think that relationships are absolutely critical. The time that you take for yourself to fill your cup up outside of work is absolutely critical, and not forgetting all of the other things that you love to do outside of building your company. I think remembering that you're a full 360-degree human being has been so huge for me, especially when times get tough.

Most people never get started. What would you say to someone who has a dream but is holding back from making the plunge?

I think one of the biggest things I've learned is that sometimes what you don't know can be a huge strength. Asking for help is so huge because a lot of people are so willing to share what they know, and you can almost instantaneously build a network that way. I think that one of the most powerful things for our growth has been not being like everybody else, especially when it comes to selling our product. A lot of people go through a broker and a distributor to get into these grocery stores, but I didn't know what the right path was, so I did it my own way and went in and met these people at the store level, face-to-face, and we got in that way. I think knowing that there's not just one way to be successful and get from point A to B. Appreciate every part of the insecurity because it's an opportunity for growth.

How do you relentlessly pursue excellence, greatness, and success (however you define it), while at the same time enjoy the journey of life?

From my own health journey, I think it's put so many different things in my life into perspective. Anyone who's been through some sort of chronic illness or near-death experience or something that's been life-altering, it really shows you that tomorrow's never promised, and since tomorrow's never promised, we have to show up in the best possible way that we can today. I think one of the tough things about running a company is you do have to plan relatively far in advance, and you can't always fully live in the moment, so that balance can be tough, but I think being able to slow down and know there's always going to be more things to do and more ways to grow has been super powerful. Showing up in the best possible way you can today is going to set you up for the best possible chance of success tomorrow.

What is one action you recommend someone do every day to be the best version of themselves?

Journaling has been super transformative to me. I'm a pen and paper, old-school kind of person, and I realized through journaling that there are so many thoughts stuck in my head that I don't even consciously realize are there. When I physically get them out onto paper, I'm able to find so much more clarity, so much more peace. Even if it's a brain dump, I just need those things out of my head so I can focus on other things throughout the day. It's been so transformative to me, and I think one other thing is that time that I journal is typically thirty minutes to an hour in the morning, and I don't touch my phone at all. I wake up to my alarm and then put it away, and I think not having that instant stimulation and having that creative space for yourself really helps you to set your own thoughts for the day. I don't think we realize how much all of the things that we take in everyday impact us, so it's been huge carving out that time in the morning to be one with my thoughts.

How have relationships—personal and professional—contributed to your success and happiness?

Relationships and business are one and the same. I think that both personally and professionally, my relationships have played a huge role in my success. A lot of my mentors or advisors or investors have obviously played a very big role too, but I think beyond everything, coming at a relationship from a long-term perspective and approaching it with a ton of communication is key. I always say it's better to err on the side of over communicating than thinking someone understands something when maybe they don't. Genuine care and respect go so far, whether that's a personal relationship or professional. I love to see people win, and I want to do whatever I can to support them. When I think of the way I try to approach relationships, I like to do that for everyone in every way that I can, and it just so happens a lot of the time that's reciprocated, and it's been huge.

Who are three of your favorite entrepreneurs to follow, learn from, and/or connect with?

Sara Blakely

Oprah Winfrey

Deepak Chopra

NICK SANTONASTASSO

Bio

Nick Santonastasso is a medical miracle. Not only is he one of four people alive with the rare genetic condition, Hanhart Syndrome, the inspirational keynote speaker is also an internationally known bodybuilder and fitness model—despite missing both his legs and one arm since birth. The high-energy youth shares his amazing story, showing people that anyone can thrive if they have the determination and willpower to go after what they want. When Nick was born, the doctors handed his parents a long list of things that he would never be able to do. Nick's parents politely thanked them and threw the list out. They raised Nick the same way they had raised his three able-bodied older siblings and instilled in him never to let the world tell him what he could or couldn't do.

How to Connect

IG: @nicksantonastasso

FB: /nicksantonastasso

YT: /nicksanto534

How We Met

The dots to connect on this one brings up so many great memories. My good friend, Brian Mayoral, former Tony Robbins national speaker and peak performance strategist introduced me to Ratmir Rafikov, Nick's manager. We got to know each other and realized we all share the same ambition and thirst for greatness. I asked Ratmir if he'd be willing to check in with Nick about being in the book, and the rest is history.

What is your definition of success?

My definition of success is combining your passion, what makes you feel excited, what makes you feel fulfilled, and being able to monetize it. I don't think the majority of people really believe that they can turn their passion into profit or their passion into a business and provide for themselves when you really can. My whole version of success and work is I would much rather fall on my face and pursue something that I enjoy that fires me up than be building something that I don't enjoy or that I hate doing every day because we don't get the time back. For me, everything is about quality of life. Is this going to improve the quality of my life? Am I going to feel better each and every day pursuing this? So, my definition of success is combining what I'm passionate about and providing as much value as I can to provide financial freedom for me, myself, and my family.

How do you relentlessly pursue excellence, greatness, and success (however you define it), while at the same time enjoy the journey of life?

You have to have a roadmap. We all have goals, but you need those action steps, those things that you need to work on to learn and evolve to get you closer to your goal. Before, I wasn't really doing much traveling, and I wasn't a speaker. And then all of a sudden it blew up, and I was on the road 80–85 percent of the year. I think what helps me is self-reflecting and telling myself I'm grateful that I have things going on because I remember a time where I was sitting on my couch and I had no gigs, no bookings, no interviews, no phone calls, no meetings, and no team to lead. So, in the midst of the chaos, I always have to go back to being appreciative for all the opportunities I have in front of me because I don't know how long it's going to last, and it wasn't always like that.

What is one action you recommend someone do every day to be the best version of themselves?

You need to commit to something. It can be a big thing, or it can be a small thing. It could be reading some pages of a book every day or finishing a podcast every day. Or maybe you're more into health, and you need to evolve your health, so maybe it's drinking a gallon of water every day. But the thing is, everything stems down to your confidence, the relationship you have within yourself, how you view yourself, and how you feel about yourself. As humans, we're all guilty of committing to things and not following through. But what we don't realize, the underlying problem is when we commit to something and we don't follow through, we diminish the way we view ourselves. We diminish our word, and our word has power. Our word is very important, so if you can continuously commit to something and follow through and self-praise yourself on that, you gain confidence, and you build the relationship you have within yourself, which makes you operate better in your personal life, which makes you operate better in your business life.

If people aren't performing in a sales call, or people aren't performing in a meeting, it's because they lack confidence in what they're working on, or they lack confidence in the way that they speak, or they lack confidence in the way that they carry themselves. Everything stems down to your confidence, and so the one practical step that you can implement into your life right now is committing to something and following through. I promise you will be a different human being on the other side, and you'll feel one hundred times better about yourself because that's the most important thing.

How have relationships—personal and professional—contributed to your success and happiness?

Relationships are everything. I'm here for long-term relationships, and a lot of people are in it for the quick fix. What can I get out of this relationship? What can I get out of this podcast interview? You're one person away, you're one handshake, one networking event from changing the trajectory of your life, so you need to nurture relationships. Those are the people that are going to help you get to the next level or who know someone that can help you get to the next level. There's that famous quote, "Your network is your net worth," but it's all about the longevity of your relationships, and that means if you're trying to find a mentor or you're trying to learn from a certain person, you have to provide value to that person before you take. It's like a bank. You have to deposit something before you withdraw, and so relationships are everything. Everything stems from relationships.

ERIK SALZENSTEIN

Bio

Erik Salzenstein is the founder of ERS Coaching and the Next Level Coaching programs. Erik is a respected and sought out online business coach and keynote speaker with his signature talk, "From Prison to Purpose."

After serving four years in prison and transforming his life while inside, he came out looking to make his mess his message, and in under three years, Erik was able to start and scale two different online coaching businesses making up to $80k a month as well as launch his speaking business, winning the 2019 Advance Your Reach Speak Off and landing a TEDx Talk.

When he's not inspiring people from stage, Erik and his team of coaches are focused on bridging the gap for their clients by giving them the full blueprint on how to take their passion and expertise and turn it into a successful and profitable online business.

Erik has built his businesses on three core standards that he lives by and expects his team to embody and his clients to embrace, which are being heart-centered, being mission-driven, and taking massive action. His attitude of gratitude and leading with a servant's heart is magnetizing, and it shows in all that he does.

How to Connect

IG: @salzenstein
FB: /erik.salzenstein.351

How We Met

Erik and I first met at a speaker's conference the week before the pandemic lockdown began. We hit it off and stayed in touch. Over the next few months, I was evolving my business, and his business kept growing. Eventually, I worked with him, and he gave me some incredible advice that produced great results. After that, I knew I had to invite him to be part of this book.

What is the one thing that, if you knew when starting, would have accelerated your path to success?

I was super impatient at the start, so I think understanding that it's a process was something I needed to really embrace more. I was getting frustrated. I thought about quitting a couple of times, so I think patience is big.

The other big thing is data. So, if I would have gone back right from the start, I would have been more conscious about using the data to make decisions and leaning on that data to build.

What are three pieces of software/technology you recommend people use in their business?

Telegram, Voxer, Slack (ongoing communication tool)

Zoom

Google Drive

For somebody who has dreams of being a wildly successful entrepreneur with freedom, what is the most important thing to focus on?

Since you emphasized freedom, my mind went to systems and structure because I'm a big believer that more systems and more structure gives you more freedom. So, if we're emphasizing freedom not just a successful entrepreneur, then I'm going to say that we really want to put attention on your systems, on your standard operating procedures (SOPs), and on the structures that you have within your business. Once those things get built out and you hire your first person, whether it's a VA or it's whatever that role is, you now have a set of SOPs attached to that role not that person. Now there's a system in place so if that person gets removed, you're going to be able to get somebody right back in to fulfill that role with less headache, less time, less friction, and less resistance.

The question that comes next is where can I start outsourcing and automating to remove myself from parts of the business. When you ask yourself that question, things are going to come and you're going to realize you actually don't even need to be doing certain things. You teach this idea, process, or strategy to literally every single client or you repeat yourself three times a week so now you decide this needs to be a module. Now you have a system in place for that one part of your business, and you just removed yourself from having to repeat yourself time and time again.

No entrepreneurial journey goes from A to B in a straight line. How did you overcome the internal doubts and external adversity along the journey?

It's all framing. It's looking at the opposition and recognizing it's an opportunity. It's looking at the challenge and saying, "yes this is real, this is a roadblock, there's friction here, there's resistance here, but this is meant for me, and I'm so grateful for this challenge. I'm so grateful for this heartache because it's going to make me a better person." Any time that you're faced with resistance, know that you're right on the cusp of growth and change. Then it's about actually taking the action to reframe it to serve you instead of hurt you. It's all about framing.

What is your definition of success?

For me, my big why for growing both of my businesses was retiring my mom and getting her out of the nine to five. She was married for thirty years before she and my dad got divorced. My parents are both great people, but my mom had to go back to work, so at seventy years old, she's been answering the phone for the last nine years at a dermatologist office. My big why for being a successful, profitable entrepreneur was retiring her. She went from forty hours a week to now four hours a week with me. So that big why was accomplished.

My new big why is giving back. Right now, my version of success is being able to just wildly give. I just want to be able to give, give, give. To me, that really represents when I've reached success. The more I can give, the more success I have.

How do you relentlessly pursue excellence, greatness, and success (however you define it), while at the same time enjoy the journey of life?

This is where the balance comes in, and this is something that I'm working on and something I have to remind myself. Right after this, I'm going for a walk because I've been working all morning and afternoon, but I need to go reset right now. I need to get some sun, and I need to go free my mind. I'm going to take a thirty-minute walk with the dog. I think it's balance and knowing when to unplug and cut off. That's stuff that I've had to learn and still am learning how to do because I love what I do. I can constantly work. I can work nonstop, and it's arguably not the healthiest thing to do, and so I think setting clear boundaries is super important. It's something I'm challenged with and continuing to improve on.

What is one action you recommend someone do every day to be the best version of themselves?

Deep work. You have to have an hour of deep work minimum. Deep work in the sense of work that is truly moving the needle in your business, not busy work. This is work that is truly moving the needle, whatever that is, for whatever stage that you're at, but you have to have an hour of phone on airplane mode and no distractions.

Then I would also say that whatever space you're in, you should be spending thirty minutes to an hour a day, five days a week minimum, mastering your craft. Let's say you're a fitness coach and you hired a business coach. The business coach is helping you with the marketing, and he's helping you with all the business things, and you're taking all the action. You should still be spending thirty minutes to an hour a day learning from another fitness coach who's further ahead of you, who has knowledge or skills that you don't have. You have to be sharpening your sword. You have to be mastering your craft because you're going to have more value to give your people, and you're going to have more confidence in how you're showing up. You're also going to be more motivated because every time you sit down and read that person's stuff or see someone further along than you, it's going to excite you and push you to show up stronger in your own business. It's not just getting the tools and strategies to grow the business; it's also making sure that you're still plugged in to how to be a better coach in whatever space you're in or whatever it is that you do.

How have relationships—personal and professional—contributed to your success and happiness?

I will never in a million years say I'm self-made. I will never use those words. You're responsible for your success. At the end of the day, success is my responsibility, but everybody who's played a role in my life contributed something. They held me accountable, they pushed me, they gave me a new opportunity, they gave me a new strategy and not just in the sense of getting but also giving. It's me giving to other people because it's other people that have given me the opportunity to present to them a strategy or a process. It's those people that have allowed me to be at this level, so my mindset when I got out of prison was how can I constantly look to add value. Where can I add more value? How can I add more value? It was always adding value. That was my entire framework on life. When I was a server at two restaurants, I thought, "How can I make this a better dining experience for the customers. How can I go above and beyond for my customers? What can I do as a server that they don't expect and they don't get from these other servers? How can I separate myself from all the others?"

It's constantly looking to whatever relationship you're in and asking, "How can I add more value to this relationship?" It's making sure that you're also plugging yourself in with people who think the same, people who are giving, and when you leave their presence, you're feeling better, more energized, and more motivated. Those are the people that you want to be around.

Who are three of your favorite entrepreneurs to follow, learn from, and/or connect with?

Taki Moore

Todd Brown

Vince Del Monte

Craig Ballantyne

Zander Fryer

MARLEY JAXX

Bio

Marley Jaxx is the CEO of Jaxx Productions and a highly acclaimed business acceleration coach. From the pages of *Forbes* to the main stage at Funnel Hacking Live, Marley works with her clients to create an evergreen content machine and predictable cashflow system inside their business, a.k.a. the most proven, guru-hidden, cashflow system built on effortless high-ticket customer ascension.

How to Connect

IG: @marleyjaxx

YT: /marleyjaxx

Website: marleyjaxx.com

How We Met

I first heard of Marley through the ClickFunnels community. After seeing her name show up time and time again, I reached out to her via IG DM. We chatted for a bit, and then I invited her to be part of my summit. I loved our interview, and we stayed in touch. When I was looking for guests for the book, Marley was an obvious choice, so I messaged her to see if she was interested, and here we are.

What is the one thing that, if you knew when starting, would have accelerated your path to success?

I didn't know at the time that business was more than just "something you do." It's such a game of personal development. I love Alex Charfen's quote that "if you don't have the business you want, it's because you haven't become the person who can run it yet." So much of my business growth has come after times where I've been challenged or worked through a lot of resistance. My business evolves as I do, so now it's my responsibility to continue to work on my self-awareness and personal development. I probably would have done more personal therapy than courses and trainings.

What are three pieces of software/technology you recommend people use in their business?

ClickFunnels

Voxer

Scribd (Netflix for books)

For somebody who has dreams of being a wildly successful entrepreneur with freedom, what is the most important thing to focus on?

Personal development and relationships. Your network is your net worth, and your self-worth being generated from within is a solid foundation to work from with authenticity. I think all entrepreneurs start their business from a place of having something to prove. This is good for a time; it serves us and can be a strong motivator, but at some point, we (hopefully) come to a place of wondering what else there is to life to make it more meaningful. Then our fuel switches from pain to passion or purpose. You'll be much more successful and fulfilled there.

What is your definition of success?

Fulfillment in the effort, not the attainment of my goals. Being inspired by what I get to create every day and doing it with people I love. Freedom: time freedom, financial freedom, creative freedom.

Most people never get started. What would you say to someone who has a dream but is holding back from making the plunge?

Your excuses or whatever you tell yourself is the reason you're holding yourself back probably isn't the real reason. If you wait until you're "ready," you'll never be ready. Do it scared and be honest and transparent about your fears. Your vulnerability will make others feel safe and maybe even give them permission to do what scares them when they see you as an example. I remember one night I was alone in an Airbnb after a mastermind I paid way more than I could even afford at the time. I was crying at the table and having a serious heart to heart with myself, telling myself I couldn't play small anymore. I owed it to myself and the audience waiting for me to step up. It wasn't smooth sailing from there, the fears and imposter syndrome were always there and still are. At each level you progress, it's "new level, new devil." The challenges don't go away, they just evolve as you do. But I made a commitment to myself, and commitment means getting up and playing even when you're hurt. It means not taking your successes or your failures personally. It means getting up and doing it anyway, even when you *feel* tired or *feel* scared, because commitment doesn't care how you feel.

How do you relentlessly pursue excellence, greatness, and success (however you define it), while at the same time enjoy the journey of life?

"Satisfaction lies in the effort not in the attainment." When being challenged, I remind myself that I love this game and that I signed up for this. As an entrepreneur, I've signed up for a lifestyle of constant transition, overcoming resistance, and evolving in my self-awareness. I also remind myself of everything I've experienced to get to where I am now. It's so much easier to connect the dots looking backwards. Instead of looking at it as a challenge, I choose to view it as an adventure with deep curiosity: What will happen next? Where will I go from here? Who will I be tomorrow?

What is one action you recommend someone do every day to be the best version of themselves?

Another Alex Charfen quote: "Self-care is the gateway to success." Self-care can look different for everyone. It could be meditating, journaling, a bubble bath, Netflix, or pizza, but one that has been most important to me is to move your body. Not just for health or fitness but for creativity. I wouldn't consider myself an athlete, I don't play sports, I am not a runner, but when I feel present in my body and have spent the time connecting with this vehicle I get to do life with, I feel like a conduit. Imagine it even on a cellular level: buzzing, energetic, centered. I'm ready to play and create.

How have relationships—personal and professional—contributed to your success and happiness?

Audrey Hepburn had a quote: "I have an enormous need for affection and a terrible need to give it." I don't want to take for granted that I turned my hobby into a business, and I get to choose the incredibly talented people I am lucky enough to do it with. When people ask what I do for fun outside of work, I have a hard time answering that question. I do what I love with the people I love. I strive to have intimacy and depth in my personal relationships and my professional relationships. I learn so much from the people I surround myself with. Their contribution in my life has been life changing, and I hope that I can provide the same for them.

Who are three of your favorite entrepreneurs to follow, learn from, and/or connect with?

Alex Charfen

Stephen Larsen

Leila Hormozi

FUN FACTS ABOUT THE GUESTS

I am a huge math nerd. I absolutely love math, and I love looking at the numbers to inform my decisions. That being said, here are some fun facts and stats about the creation of this book and the guests who are featured.

Out of the thirty-nine people interviewed and featured, fourteen of them participated as a result of cold outreach, twelve of them were introductions from other guests/friends, and thirteen of them were people I already knew or had at least talked to once before.

Let's dig into this a bit further.

Six of the fourteen people I reached out to through cold outreach have over 100,000 followers on Instagram.

What does this mean?

People are more accessible than you think. Just because you see a blue checkmark or a ton of followers doesn't mean they are any less human. Sure, it might require you to be more creative, but with the right approach, you can connect with a lot of amazing people.

Of the twelve people I was introduced to, all of them said yes without hesitation. Why? The power of an introduction is huge.

While we want to believe that we have to build on our own, people want to help you. People want to see you succeed. People want to introduce great people to each other.

Always make sure you deliver incredible value and always make sure you ask for help because people will always help you if it creates great opportunities for themselves or for the people they care about.

The greatest way to build your network is to create something of value. When I was thinking of what I could do to really stand out, I decided to go big. I decided to spend hundreds of hours and literally write a book to grow my network and meet people I've looked up to for years.

Some of the people I featured in the book have sold hundreds of thousands of books and made millions of dollars. So, what made me different from everyone else who wanted to get their attention and build a relationship?

I created something of incredible value and excitement, and you can too!

No matter where you are in your journey, you have something of value to add. You just have to figure out what it is. As the great Les Brown once said, "You must be willing to do the things today others won't do in order to have the things tomorrow others won't have."

BJ FOGG

Bio

BJ Fogg, PhD, founded the Behavior Design Lab at Stanford University. In addition to his research, Fogg teaches industry innovators how human behavior really works. He created the Tiny Habits Academy to help people around the world. He lives in Northern California and Maui.

Find out more at BJFogg.com and visit TinyHabits.com to learn about his New York Times best-selling book, *Tiny Habits: The Small Changes that Change Everything.*

How to Connect

Website: bjfogg.com & tinyhabits.com

How We Met

I read BJ's book, *Tiny Habits: The Small Changes that Change Everything* (you should read it), and I absolutely loved it! I decided that after reading his book, we needed to be friends or at least have a conversation. I started doing my research and found that professionals can apply to have a fifteen-minute chat with BJ. My request was approved, and we jumped on a fifteen-minute call. During that call, I came prepared with unique and valuable questions for him to answer, and I talked about something personal that I found we had in common. At the end of our fifteen-minutes, I asked if he'd be interested in being featured in my book. He said yes, and we made it happen.

What is the one thing that, if you knew when starting, would have accelerated your path to success?

Realizing that the Fogg Behavior Model was absolutely the right solution for how human behavior works. In 2007 it was hard for me to understand how correct this answer is to the long-standing riddle about how human behavior works.

The Fogg Behavior Model (behaviormodel.org)

A behavior happens when three things come together at the same moment - motivation, ability and a prompt for that behavior. If any one is missing, the behavior won't happen.

For somebody who has dreams of being a wildly successful entrepreneur with freedom, what is the most important thing to focus on?

I'll give you two things. I call them maxims, and this is in my book, *Tiny Habits*. It's so important.

Fogg Maxim #1: Help people do what they already want to do. This means you're not persuading people to do things they don't want to do. You're helping them do what they already want to do.

Fogg Maxim #2: Help people feel successful.

Those are the two keys to engagement, to lasting change, and to having a successful product and company.

What is your definition of success?

For me, it's really about helping people be happier and healthier.

Most people never get started. What would you say to someone who has a dream but is holding back from making the plunge?

People call me for help on start-ups and in big companies, so I've done thousands of phone calls, and they're free. And one of the things I tell entrepreneurs is to stop reading and start implementing. Put it into the world. The way you really learn is not by reading theory, it's by doing something. That's when you start learning, so stop reading and start doing.

How do you relentlessly pursue excellence, greatness, and success (however you define it), while at the same time enjoy the journey of life?

I create habits. I'm living in Maui right now and this morning, even though it was cold from a Maui standpoint, I went out surfing. One of the habits I've created goes like this. After I get to the water's edge, I will stop and pause and recommit that day to serving as many people in the best way that I can. Creating habits like this helps me feel like I'm doing the best I can.

How have relationships—personal and professional— contributed to your success and happiness?

A lot. Anybody who's written a book knows that even though your name is on the cover, it's a huge team that has helped you get there. In fact, the dedication of my book is to those people who have inspired me to explore. There are people I have relationships with including my Sunday School teacher from when I was eight, Donna McLelland. I call her out because even at that young age I saw this model of what a teacher could be, what a teacher could do, and how a teacher could be so transformative. Yes, I research and discover things, but that's not useful if I'm not teaching it and sharing it.

Who are three of your favorite entrepreneurs to follow, learn from, and/or connect with?

Reid Hoffman

David Weekly

Manu Kumar

KARA GOLDIN

Bio

Kara Goldin is the founder and CEO of Hint, Inc., best known for its award-winning Hint water, the leading unsweetened flavored water.

She has received numerous accolades, including being named EY Entrepreneur of the Year 2017 Northern California and one of *InStyle's* 2019 Badass 50. Previously, Kara was VP of Shopping Partnerships at America Online. She hosts the podcast *The Kara Goldin Show*. Her first book, *Undaunted: Overcoming Doubts and Doubters,* was released October 2020 and is now a WSJ and Amazon Best Seller. Kara lives in the Bay Area with her family.

How to Connect
IG: @karagoldin

FB: /karagoldin

LI: /karagoldin

TW: @karagoldin

How We Met

When I created The Elevation Summit, I reached out to Kara to have her be part of the summit. Unfortunately, the timing didn't work out and she couldn't participate. A few months went by, and I kept seeing her name over and over again. I decided that I needed to try again and bring a new opportunity her way, so I invited her to be in the book. Over a few DMs and emails, we locked in a time and boom, made it happen!

What is the one thing that, if you knew when starting, would have accelerated your path to success?

I think relying on myself and being more confident in my own abilities. I kept looking for a person or industry expert who was super experienced to wave their magic wand, throw the fairy dust on, and make everything perfect. I think that if I would have just said that I'm capable of figuring this out and taking it one step at a time, it would have been a faster process. When I started saying, "Hey, I can do this," that's living undaunted.

For somebody who has dreams of being a wildly successful entrepreneur with freedom, what is the most important thing to focus on?

I think not making your goal so giant that it becomes unattainable. Now, I think it's fine to have big dreams, but I always share with people who want to be entrepreneurs that ideas are a dime a dozen because a true great entrepreneur and visionary is one that can actually come up with the idea and then kickstart that idea to get it going. They figure out what things that they need to do first and also build a team to actually continue expanding on that. When you think about dreams, people will come up with these giant dreams, and they won't actually go do them because they seem so difficult and so big, but they just don't really know where to start. I think that the key thing is, it's fine to have a big dream, but being able to break it into little steps ultimately gets you where you want to go.

What is your definition of success?

Enjoying what you're doing.

How do you relentlessly pursue excellence, greatness, and success (however you define it), while at the same time enjoy the journey of life?

You just never make what you're doing so big that you can't enjoy it. I think you have to be open to exploration along the way and know that while maybe you're setting out to attain some kind of success and enjoy that success, there'll be little things along the way that you should pick up on that ultimately will lead to the ultimate success. There are little things along the way that you have to cherish to really enjoy it.

What is one action you recommend someone do every day to be the best version of themselves?

Feed your body with all of the right things. Not only with what you're drinking, obviously water or a product like Hint plus healthy food, but also really having a positive mindset and enjoying what you're doing. Call it success or call it a positive mindset, but I think that really starts with appreciating everything that's around you, not only the people but also what you're reading and what you're doing every single day.

How have relationships—personal and professional— contributed to your success and happiness?

I think relationships are everything. Being a creative, inquisitive, and curious person, the relationships that I really seek are ones where there is a loop. There's a constant give and take along the way, and it's interesting because I would say that even during a pandemic when I'm not able to see all the people that I want to see, I'm still the kind of person that can pick up the phone. And those relationships are still super strong. I think when you find friendships that are not one way or relationships that are not one way, it ultimately leads to so much more happiness.

Who are three of your favorite entrepreneurs to follow, learn from, and/or connect with?

Steve Jobs

Gregg Renfrew

Gary Vaynerchuk

Julie Wainwright

Adam Grant

Samantha Ettus

Joe Polish

Susan McPherson

BROCK JOHNSON

Bio

Brock Johnson is a twenty-four-year-old former college athlete with a passion for helping others grow their brands using social media. His specialty is short-form video on Instagram and online storytelling! After less than two years in business, Brock reached a six-figure income as a college student. As co-host of the *Build Your Tribe* podcast, instructor of multiple online courses, viral TikTok creator, and an Instagram marketing expert, Brock has helped thousands of entrepreneurs learn to build their business, even with limited time and money. He has a specialty in IG Stories, and his mission is to help you grow your brand and effectively market using these platforms.

How to Connect
IG: @brock11johnson
Website: instaclubhub.prupel.com

How We Met

When I first heard of Brock, I loved that he was a former football player. Anytime I find athletes turned entrepreneurs, I always try to reach out because we have so much in common. After a few exchanges and seeing Brock's content over the course of five months, I invited him via DM to be part of the book because I knew he would have a ton to add.

What is the one thing that, if you knew when starting, would have accelerated your path to success?

For me, it would have been reaching out and getting help. Honestly, I think the biggest thing that I've ever seen help my own business grow is hiring a virtual team. I'm in the process right now of expanding that team, and I can say that every single time that I have brought someone new into my team, whether it's a virtual assistant, a podcast manager, or a YouTube editor, my success grows. My freedom becomes that much larger, and I'm able to make more income and spend less time sitting behind the desk and actually working. I can spend more time doing what I love to do like traveling and being with my family. If I could go back to day one in my business, I would tell myself to start hiring more people sooner.

What are three pieces of software/technology you recommend people use in their business?

Email management software

Smartphone

Microsoft To-Do

You don't necessarily need the most high-ticket or the most advanced system. You just need to find the system that works for you, and a lot of times it's going to be the built-in user-friendly systems that are created for all of us to use these different services and software.

For somebody who has dreams of being a wildly successful entrepreneur with freedom, what is the most important thing to focus on?

I think for me it's to remember my why and to remember why it is that I'm doing what I'm doing because when you forget that, you start to focus on things like vanity metrics (how many followers do I have, how well is this post doing, how many likes did I get), or you start having imposter syndrome (am I good enough, there's other people out there who are doing it better), or you start focusing on those other people and comparing yourself to them (why do they have more followers than I do, why are they showing up on all these different social media platforms when I can barely show up consistently on this one social media platform). For me and for most entrepreneurs I've talked to, their why is their family, creating financial freedom for themselves, or serving their audience.

No entrepreneurial journey goes from A to B in a straight line. How did you overcome the internal doubts and external adversity along the journey?

I've had a million different businesses in my life, and I've learned that whatever business I'm doing right now probably won't be exactly what I'm doing a couple of years from now. When I go into it with that mindset, I'm able to evolve and pivot and adapt and change as the world changes, as my passions and interests change, as markets change, as my audience changes. Those things will always change. Life is ever evolving. The only constant is change. When I go into it with the mindset of "This is what I'm doing right now, and I'm going to pour into this right now, and when things change, I will also be ready to adapt and change." I think that adaptability is one of the greatest abilities entrepreneurs can have. I've owned little businesses and sold things since I was twelve years old, and they've looked vastly different. Even if you look at my business four or five years ago, it looks vastly different than how it looks right now, but along the way, I've learned lessons. I've failed time and time again. I've pivoted and adapted and changed, but without ever getting started, I would have never ended up where I am here today.

What is your definition of success?

My definition of success is when I have found joy in doing what I'm doing and I'm totally content in my life. When people hear the word content, they think that means that you're not going for more, you're not striving for more, you're just kind of settling, and I think that there's a big difference between settling and settled. I want my soul to be settled. When my soul is settled and I'm totally content with my life and I find joy in the process of whatever it is I'm doing, that's success to me.

How do you relentlessly pursue excellence, greatness, and success (however you define it), while at the same time enjoy the journey of life?

It's trying as hard as I possibly can to forget about the outcome, to forget about the end result, to not look at the bottom line. I know it's appealing for entrepreneurs to look at the gross income statements and to look at the total number of new customers and to do the math and to break down how much money they're making per day and per year. But at the end of the day, if you focus on the day-by-day processes, the routines, the habits of success, you're able to stay present, and the rest of that will take care of itself.

What is one action you recommend someone do every day to be the best version of themselves?

Spend time in silence—whether that's meditation, prayer, journaling, or reflection. If anyone follows me on social media, this might sound crazy, because they know I'm hyped up on Mountain Dew from the moment I wake up in the morning. I always have music blasting, I'm dancing and moving around, hopping from call to call to meeting, and I'm always producing content. The best thing that I can do for myself and the number one smallest action that I would recommend you do on a daily basis is spend time in silence. How you do it is going to be different for every person, but whatever works for you, works for you. Spending some time in quiet reflection is extremely beneficial.

How have relationships—personal and professional—contributed to your success and happiness?

They always say it's not what you know but who you know. I can't attest to that enough professionally. Whether you look at it from a really tangible sense from someone else who I built a relationship with on Instagram who then gives me a shout out which then I get a couple followers from, that is direct tangible growth that has come from a relationship that I built. I can also talk about the countless mentorships and learning that has taken place from these different relationships, and I think that's another really cool thing about the era that we live in. In the past, you would have had to live in close proximity to one of these experts to build a relationship with them and get to know them and learn from them. Now, there's podcasts, YouTube channels, and social media channels where you can really feel like you have a close, intimate relationship with celebrities, influencers, and experts all over the world. You can even get some of these people to comment back and forth with you or direct message back and forth with you which can really propel your professional growth onwards.

Speaking about personal growth for a second, I think back to life as a college football player and my team and my coaches and how important those roles were and how my life totally shifted because of who my college football coaches were. You can talk about how every single one of us, and no matter what role our parents had in our lives or whoever raised us, we wouldn't be the people we are today if it wasn't for those people and the direct impact and role that they had on you.

People say that you are the average of your five closest friends, and I think that's what's really beautiful about the day and time that we live in. You're not just tied to the five people who live in your town or who are closest to you. There can be people who have a way stronger impact and influence on your life, who you've never met, via podcast, via a book that you've read, via a social media channel that you follow or subscribe to. Those kinds of people can have a way bigger impact on your life then someone who lives close to you and just happens to be one of your close friends.

Who are three of your favorite entrepreneurs to follow, learn from, and/or connect with?

Pat Flynn

Sean Cannell

Chalene Johnson

KAYLEIGH CHRISTINA

Bio

Kayleigh Christina is a published author, holistic nutritionist, and co-founder and COO of CLEARSTEM Skincare. She is committed to making a positive impact and inspiring people to become the best possible versions of themselves.

How to Connect

IG: @kayleighchristina

Website: clearstemskincare.com

How We Met

Kayleigh and I met when I launched The Elevation Summit. She had a bunch of friends speaking in the summit and reached out. Immediately, we became friends, and I added her to our speaker list. Since then, we've stayed in touch making intros for each other, so when the time came for this book, I knew she'd be a great fit. All it took to make this happen was a single text after a year of building a relationship.

What is the one thing that, if you knew when starting, would have accelerated your path to success?

Get set up with the correct manufacturers, 3PLs, and shipment warehouse centers. These are big foundational pieces when you go from self-packing and fulfilling to outsourcing. There were a lot of learning curves that we had when choosing manufacturers and 3PLs, and we got completely bulldozed financially by some of them. Making the right decisions would have helped us scale a little bit faster and not lose as much money during that time. Looking back, the best way to avoid this would have been to ask more questions and get a lot more referrals.

For somebody who has dreams of being a wildly successful entrepreneur with freedom, what is the most important thing to focus on?

Your time. When you're growing as an entrepreneur, your time is your most valuable asset, because in the beginning, you can't delegate to people as much as you would with a nine to five job that has a lot of different departments. You're typically a startup. You're either bootstrapping it or going the investor or fundraising route to get some full-time employees, but a lot of people are used beyond their bandwidth. Make the most out of your time not only for yourself, but also how you give back to others. There are different sacrifices you're going to have to make. You're going to have to say no in order to grow and move the needle on your business. A good way to measure time is to take a look at your daily and weekly schedule and see where you can eliminate time-wasters that are not working towards your goal.

What is your definition of success?

Finding joy in what you do and the person you are. Monday isn't my driving factor for success. We have a startup, and I've never attached my success to income or compared myself to what someone else is making. As long as I feel comfortable enough to live and go on fun adventures, I'm happy. Truly waking up, excited to do what I do every single morning feels successful to me. There are benchmarks I want to hit along the way which are really cool, but those only give you a little spike in serotonin. It gives you that happy moment, but success is doing what makes you happy every single day—finding joy in the small things, spending time with the people you love, and creating that long-term feeling of happiness and success.

Most people never get started. What would you say to someone who has a dream but is holding back from making the plunge?

You honestly just have to start somewhere. I think some people think they need to give up everything in life to start a company, and that does work with some people. Some people need to feel such pressure that they have no choice but to succeed in order to start something. There are other people like me who worked a full-time corporate job for a long time while building CLEARSTEM on the side because financial stability was very important for my stress levels. I felt like I couldn't give my all to CLEARSTEM if I was too worried about my living situation, finances, etc. It's okay to have slower growth, build on the side, give up some mornings, evenings, and weekends to build your dream while still staying stable and in your full-time job.

How do you relentlessly pursue excellence, greatness, and success (however you define it), while at the same time enjoy the journey of life?

We definitely have big goals that I want to hit—big revenue goals, big team goals, big collaboration goals—and those do genuinely make me really happy seeing the needle move with the business. That is very, very important to me. One of my best friends, Kacia Fitzgerald, has really put things into perspective for me. There have been so many times where I barely get excited about little things. I'd always be asking, "What's the next goal? What's the next goal?" She'd tell me to stop, take a step back, and ask if we could celebrate this. Celebrate what's happening now in the moment.

I quickly move past things, so I had to make a conscious effort myself to celebrate my wins, to stop and enjoy them. I also think you should celebrate the times where you've overcome a major challenge. That's almost bigger to celebrate than a feature in a magazine.

What is one action you recommend someone do every day to be the best version of themselves?

Journaling and drinking water. Drinking water as the very first thing when you get up, because if caffeine is the first thing that you drink, you are killing your adrenal glands, which release your stress hormones. So, if you drink water first, you are protecting those stress hormones. Secondly, journaling. And it doesn't have to be crazy, but I think positive affirmations and reflecting on a positive experience in the last twenty-four hours helps prime your brain to see the positive in that next day. So, when things are thrown at you, your brain is a little more ready and prepared to handle what could go wrong and help you take a step back and see the positive. I have a five-minute journaling routine I do every morning that helps set the tone for the rest of the day.

How have relationships—personal and professional—contributed to your success and happiness?

Friendships are so incredibly important to me because friendships are built on vulnerability, honesty, and connection, and I've truly built an incredible group of friends where we all understand each other. A lot of them are entrepreneurs, so we struggle with a lot of the same things. As entrepreneurs, we struggle with different things than people with nine to five jobs. There are no pros and cons to either, but it's very different when it comes to stress, time management, relationships, and commitments. That is why it's so important to surround myself with an amazing group of people that are there to talk me through things, help pick me up if I'm ever feeling down, and of course celebrate the wins.

Who are three of your favorite entrepreneurs to follow, learn from, and/or connect with?

Brandin Cohen

Samantha Pantazopoulos

Sara Blakely

HOW TO ELEVATE FURTHER

Book Bonuses

As part of investing in this book, you have unlocked access to some free bonuses.

Theelevatedentrepreneur.co/bonus

4-Step GAME Method to Consistent Leads and Sales on Social Media

This free training focuses on the core fundamentals that will help you build a profitable online business no matter the industry.

Theelevatedentrepreneur.co/game

Client Results

If you are curious what kind of results you can expect from working with us and thinking like an Elevated Entrepreneur, I've compiled some screenshots and videos from just a few of our clients to celebrate their wins.

Theelevatedentrepreneur.co/success

Join Us in Elite Elevation

If you would like some help from me and my team to implement, execute, and elevate your business, we'd love to invite you to chat with us.

Head over to theelevatedentrepreneur.co/apply

There will be a few questions so we can better get to know you and your business. Once that is complete, you will be able to schedule a call with me and our team.

ACKNOWLEDGMENTS

I want to give a huge thank you to everyone who has helped me get to where I am today. I'm so incredibly blessed to have friends and family all over the world, and every time I write a book, I am reminded how connected we truly are.

To everyone who was gracious enough to allow me to feature you in this book, thank you. Whether we are a brand-new friend or have known each other for years, your interest and support in this book will always be appreciated. Thank you for being part of the mission to elevate.

I'd like to thank my family, specifically my parents, Dave and Sheri, and my brother, Jonah, for always supporting me on my crazy adventures. I love you guys so much!

I'd like to thank my assistant, Emma Roberts, for helping me create this book. This book is unlike a traditional book as not only did you help me with feedback, organization, and writing, but you helped coordinate with hundreds of people to make sure everything was accurate. I appreciate the effort and energy you gave to this book.

I want to give a big shoutout to Jordan Cuellar for designing the cover of this book. Your work is incredible, and I am blessed to have you on our team.

To my editor, Carly Catt. Thank you for being amazing and working with me so closely on this book. I appreciate your skills, and I'm so grateful for your help in making this book come to life.

And of course, to you, the readers. Thank you for making the choice to elevate with me. I appreciate your time, energy, and attention. Thank you for allowing me to play a part in your journey to greatness.